Homing with
The Birds

GENE STRATTON-PORTER

Homing with the birds, G. Stratton-Porter
Jazzybee Verlag Jürgen Beck
86450 Altenmünster, Loschberg 9
Deutschland

ISBN: 9783849689001

www.jazzybee-verlag.de
www.facebook.com/jazzybeeverlag
admin@jazzybee-verlag.de

Printed by Createspace, North Charleston, SC, USA

CONTENTS:

INTRODUCTION

IN THE fall of 1916, while visiting at the home of Mr. F. N. Doubleday, a member of the house which publishes most of my books, in conversation with my very dear friend Mrs. Neltje De Graff Doubleday, the author of a number of invaluable books on birds and flowers, she began to question me about unusual experiences I encountered afield. I told her some of the things here recorded, the queerest and most peculiar things that I had seen during a lifetime of personal contact with the birds. In the course of that intimate conversation, Mrs. Doubleday conceived and planned this book, feeling – I hope not mistakenly – that these intimate personal experiences with birds, which so intensely interested her, would not fail to be of equal interest to other bird lovers and protectors. She felt that these records faithfully and simply set down would add very largely to the sum of human achievement in a scientific estimate of the habits and characteristics of birds. So, I have written for any one who is interested, these sketches of personal experience, as I outlined them to such a devoted lover and champion of the birds as Neltje Blanchan.

CHAPTER I - EARNING A TITLE

ALMOST my first distinct memory is connected with a bird. I found a woodpecker lying on the grass beneath a cherry tree. I could not understand why he did not fly with the birds flocking over the fruit; I spread his wings and tossed him through the air, but he only fell to the ground. Then I noticed that his kind were all flying from the tree tops and high places, so I carried him upstairs and launched him from a window. He fell as before. Then I thought perhaps he was hungry; I took him to the garden, pried open his beak, and stuffed him with green gooseberries, but still he would not fly. In complete discouragement, I sat on the front steps with the bird in my lap, wondering what I could do to help him. My father passed, so I began asking questions. That morning I learned a new word; I had not known "dead" before. Father very carefully explained that he never permitted robins, orioles, or any song bird to be killed, but that woodpeckers made no music, while they carried away distressingly large quantities of fruit. It was then that I made my first business proposition: "If you will make the boys stop shooting woodpeckers, I will not eat another cherry. The birds may have all of mine."

My father said that was a bargain. I never before noticed that cherries were so big, so red, so tempting, while it seemed that all of our family, helpers, and friends spent most of their time offering them to me. Our cook almost broke my heart by baking a little cherry pie in a scalloped tartpan for me. I could not say a word, but I put my hands behind me and backed away from that awful temptation with tears in my eyes. At that point my mother intervened. She said she had decided that we had cherries enough for all of our needs and for the birds as well, so she gave me the pie.

It is probable that this small sacrifice on my part set me to watching and thinking about the birds, which every day flashed their bright colors and sang their unceasing songs all over and around us. For years one pair of wrens homed over the kitchen door, the entrance to their dwelling being a knot hole in the upper casing. While the mother bird brooded the father frequently spent an hour at a time, often in the rain, on a wooden acorn ornamenting the top of the pump on our back porch, becoming so tame that he frequently brushed us with his wings in going back and forth to his door, sometimes alighting on our heads. In his behalf I spent much time sweeping up the debris dropped by the pair on the back porch while building their nest, because my mother threatened to nail shut the opening; but as she never did, I strongly suspect that she had no real intention of so doing.

She was a great friend of a pair of hummingbirds that almost always nested in a honeysuckle over her bedroom window. One day, the front door having been left open, the male bird flew into the room and did not seem able to find his way out again. When he had circled the ceiling, striking his head until the feathers were worn away and tiny touches of red began to show on the paper, my mother could endure no more; so she summoned help and finally succeeded in capturing the bird, which she allowed me to hold in my hands while she showed me how small its body was, how tiny its feet, how fine its bill.

She had much trouble with the swifts that built in the chimney to a huge fireplace in our living room. A number of these birds would build their nests near the top of this chimney every season, beginning a raucous chatter very early in the morning, constantly dropping twigs and clay over the andirons and into the fireplace; while, either from imperfect construction or through heavy rains loosening the fastenings, there never was a season that one or more nests did not fall into the fireplace, frequently carrying young birds almost ready for flight with them. They were very seldom killed in the fall, but they swept down soot, and flopped around in the ashes to the vexation of Mother's housewifely soul. The old birds often fell with the nests or followed down the chimney and escaped into the room; so they, too, decorated the ceiling with their blood, if they fell when we chanced to be away from home and they were not released immediately. Often, if the nest were not completely shattered, I gathered up the pieces, wired them back into shape to the best of my ability, climbed from an upstairs window to the roof of the back part of the house, which was only one story, and from there to the roof of the second story. By using pieces of shingle and bits of wire, I replaced the nests inside the chimney, then put the little birds back into them. It was a frequent prophecy with the family that I should break my neck in this undertaking.

My experience with birds began as soon as I could walk, at my home, Hopewell Farm, in Wabash County, Indiana. As I recall our farm at that time, it was of unusual beauty, a perfect inland location for birds. The public highway ran north and south through the middle of the land. On the west of the road were a number of cultivated fields and one large tract of native timber. On the east of the road lay the residence, surrounded by a large, tree-filled dooryard, south of which was a garden, bright with flowers and shrubs. Behind the dooryard spread a very large orchard filled with apple trees and bordered with peach trees on three sides, with rare peach, plum, and pear trees on the fourth. A lane ran from the barnyard to a woods pasture where much of the heavy timber had been cut away leaving only a few large trees interspersed with berry bushes and thickets of wild-rose and elder. Three streams of running water crossed the place, one flowing through the woods and rounding the foot of a steep hill south of the residence. A smaller one flowed in a parallel direction on the north, both emptying into a larger stream coming from the north through our meadow and joining the Wabash River several miles south of us.

The land was new, a large part of it having been cleared and put into cultivation by my father. All of the wild growth was much ranker and more luxuriant than at the present time, while this was true also of everything we cultivated. My mother used the natural fertilizer from the poultry house and stable in her garden; the cleanings from the barn were scattered over the fields; but no other fertilizer ever was talked of at that time.

The flowers and all growth were more luxuriant than now because the soil was young, the temperature more equable. Summer always brought heavy rains every few days; long periods of heat and drought and cyclones or high, raging winds were unknown. As I recall, there were small flocks of birds for every one that is seen at the present time. We were taught to love the song birds for their beauty, their music, and the likeness of their life processes to ours. We were told that we must not harm a bird's nest because it would break the little mother bird's heart; but no one ever particularly impressed it upon us to protect them because the berry and fruit crops would fail if we did not. My father was the only person I ever heard mention the subject in my childhood. The birds' work as insect exterminators was not generally realized or taught at that time, while the spraying of fruit trees was unknown. When the trees had been pruned and the trunks given a thorough coat of whitewash, everything that was known to do for their care had been done; and so bounteous and fine were the fruit crops in my father's orchard that the whitewash was not used there, but I did see it in neighboring orchards and dooryards.

I distinctly remember the swarms of birds that flocked over the cherry trees when the fruit was ripe, and the Babel of song that went up from the orchard, while the field birds were so numerous that we were always allowed to take the eggs from any quail nest we found, provided we first used the precaution of raking one egg from the nest with a long stick to see to what stage of incubation it had progressed. If the quail had not finished laying or had brooded only a few hours, we carried the eggs to the house, put them in cold water, boiled them for twelve minutes, let them cool in the water, and divided them among the children, as one of the greatest treats possible. No other egg I ever have tasted was so fine in grain and delicate in flavor. Despite the destruction we must have wrought in a season, the quail were so numerous that it was the custom to build traps of long, fine pieces of wood, covered with leaves, and set with a trigger, baited with grain. A trail of grain led to these traps, where from half a dozen up to twelve and more of the birds frequently imprisoned themselves at one time. The advantage over shooting was that the birds were in perfect condition when taken. Now, this seems a dreadful thing to have done, but at that time quail were so plentiful we never could distinguish any diminution in their numbers, while rabbits and squirrels were pests, which we had to fight to protect our fruit trees and for our comfort. After the cold weather set in at Thanksgiving time, we always had a large supply of frozen quail and rabbits hanging in the smokehouse for a treat upon the arrival of unexpected guests.

The only game bird, the protection of which I ever heard mentioned in my childhood, was the wild pigeon. My father never would allow our boys to go to the pigeon roosts, baffle the birds with the light of lanterns, club them, and carry them away by bagfuls, as some of our neighbours did. He said that such proceedings would eventually end in the extermination of the birds; that God gave us these creatures to enjoy but not to destroy; so he always cautioned all of us, either in hunting or fishing, to be content with a "moderate share." The prophecy he then made concerning the wild pigeons has found its fulfillment in my day, for a heavy reward has been offered for a number of years past for even one specimen of this beautiful bird, the metallic luster of whose plumage made a gleam of light when on wing, and whose whistling flight was familiar music in my childhood. These birds now seem to have joined the extinct starlings of Ile de la Reunion.

All of the trees and most of the bushes surrounding the house were filled with bird nests. A privet bush in one corner of the garden always had at least one nest, while the grape arbor and berry bushes sheltered many. There were little cups of hair even among the currant and gooseberry bushes. Every bird that ever homed in an orchard in the Central States was to be found in the apple trees, in a big heap of trimmings at the back of the orchard, in the hollow rails of the fence, or in the grassy corners of our orchard. I think too that every bird of the fields was to be found in our meadow, our clover fields, and in the fence corners, while the big trees of the woods pasture and of the deep woods had their share of crows, hawks, owls; while twenty years after we moved away, a pair of golden eagles nested in the woods pasture, and were shot because they were carrying off small pigs and lambs. The female of this pair is my only mounted bird.

From my earliest recollection I was the friend and devoted champion of every bird that nested in the garden, on the fences, on the ground, in the bushes, in the dooryard, or in the orchard trees. From breakfast until dinner and from dinner until supper, almost my entire day was spent in making the rounds of these nests, watching the birds while they built, brooded, or fed their young, championing their cause against other children, cats, snakes, red squirrels, or larger animals such as skunks and foxes, which were so numerous that we held organized fox-chases for their extermination.

I was always on terms of the greatest intimacy with a pewee that built on a rafter supporting the roof of a log pig-pen. It was very easy to climb from a rail fence to the roof, then by working loose a clapboard near the nest I could watch the birds' daily life and make friends with them.

I do not recall one instance during my childhood when I ever intruded myself into the affairs of any bird in such a manner as to cause it to desert its nest location. I always approached by slow degrees, remained motionless a long time, and did the birds no harm whatever; so they very soon accepted me as a part of their daily life.

One of the heartbreaks of my childhood occurred when one of our hired men forgot his instructions and put up the third bar of an opening in one of the west field fences, which I had asked Father to have him leave down, because in the opening chiseled out to hold the bar was the nest of a chippy having four exquisite, speckled eggs. When I found this bar in place and could not remove it, I hurried to my father in a tumult of grief and anger which very nearly resulted in the dismissal of the man; but it was too late to save the bird and her nest.

I can not recall how many robin nests I located in a season, but there were two locations in which the robins built where access to them was especially convenient. One was a catalpa tree in the northwest corner of our dooryard, to the branches of which I could easily step from the front picket fence. In my morning rounds I always climbed to visit this robin, sitting on a branch talking to the brooding mother bird, almost always carrying her a worm or a berry in my apron pocket as a friendship offering. The other location was the early harvest apple tree of our orchard. This tree was especially designed by nature for the convenience of children in climbing. In the first place the tree grew at an angle, and in the second it had a growth as large as a good-sized butter bowl on the top side which was in the proper position to make a first step in the ascent of the tree. We used to start a few rods away on the run, take this first step, which brought us in reach of the nearest branch, and from there we went up the tree almost as swiftly as we ran along the path. I can not recall one spring of my childhood in which the robins did not have at least one nest in this tree.

Coming from it early one summer morning I heard the crack of my father's rifle in the dooryard, then I saw a big bird whirling to earth in the milk yard, which adjoined the garden on one side, the orchard on the other. I saw my father start toward the bird, so as fast as possible I sped after him, my bare feet making no sound on the hard, worn path. A large chicken hawk was sitting back on his tail, one wing stiffly extended, the tip hanging broken and bleeding, while in the bird's eyes there was a look of commingled pain, fear, and regal defiance that drove me out of my senses. My father grasped his rifle by the barrel. As the butt came whirling around, I sprang before him and sheltered the hawk with my body, the gun whizzing past my head so close that the rush of air fanned my face. My father dragged me away.

6

"Are you mad?" he cried. "I barely missed braining you!"

"I'd rather you did hit me," I answered, "than to have you strike a bird when its eyes are like that! Oh, Father, please don't kill him! He never can fly again. Give him to me! Do please give him to me!"

"Keep back!" cried my father. "He will tear your face!"

Father was an ordained minister, better versed in Biblical history than any other man I ever have known intimately. To him, "hawk" meant "Ayit." This old Hebrew word, literally translated, means "to tear and scratch the face." That is exactly what a hawk meant to my father; the word and bird were synonymous. To me, it meant something very different, because I had watched this pair of kingly birds carry heavy sticks and limbs, with which they had built a nest in a big oak tree overhanging a bank of the brook that ran through our meadow. The structure was bigger than a bushel basket, but no one else of our family knew about it, because it was well screened by the leaves of the tree. It was part of my self-imposed, daily task to gather up from the bank skeletons of any wild bird, rabbit, or domestic fowl, which the hawks had dropped there, and consign them to the current so that the telltale evidence of their location was quickly carried down stream. I envied these birds their power to soar in the face of the wind, to ride with the stiff gale of a beating storm, or to hang motionless as if frozen in air, according to their will, as I envied nothing else on earth. I had haunted the region of this nest so long that I knew it contained a mother bird and a pair of young big enough to look down at me over the edge of the nest, while I was quite sure that the birds were as well acquainted with me as I was with them.

So, for the first time in my life, I contradicted my father.

"He won't!" I cried. "This bird knows me. He knows I would not hurt him. Oh, do please give him to me!"

To prove my assertion, I twisted from my father's grasp and laid my hands on the bird. The hawk huddled against me for protection. In a choice between a towering man who threatened with a rifle and the familiar figure of a child who offered protection, is it any wonder that the bird preferred the child? My father gazed at us in amazement.

"God knows I do not understand you," he said in all reverence. "Keep the bird, if you think you can!"

After my father had gone, the hawk began to revive from the shock. He was not so friendly as I had hoped he would be. In fact, he showed decided signs of wanting to scratch and bite. I did not know how to begin caring for him. My first thought was that he should be in a shady place, where he could have something to perch upon. I hunted a long stick and by patient maneuvering drove him to the woodhouse, where he climbed to the highest part of the corded wood. There he sat in sullen suffering for the remainder of the day. The next morning I went to him very early. I thought that after a day and a night with a broken wing and without food or drink he would surely allow me to care for him. I cautiously approached him with a basin of water. He drew back as far as he could crowd into a corner. I had always heard that wounded soldiers were frantic for water, so I patiently held the basin before the bird, dabbling and splashing to show him that it contained water. Suddenly, he thrust in his beak and drank like a famished creature. Then I offered him some scraped meat, which he finally took from the end of a stick. The flies began to cluster over the broken wing, and I knew that that must be stopped; so with one clip of the sheep shears I cut through the skin and muscle that held the dangling tip. The bird uttered a shrill scream, but he did not attack me. Then I poured cold water over the hurt wing, which was kept stiffly extended, until it was washed clean. From the time I put the cold water on, the bird ceased even to threaten me. He seemed to realize that his pain was relieved. Then I went into the house to ask my mother if there was not something in her medicine chest that would help heal the wound and keep away the flies. She thought that there was, and as she measured out a white powder for me, she smiled and said: "What a little bird woman you are!"

In two weeks, the hawk was as well as he ever could be. By that time he would take food from my fingers and allow me to do anything I chose for him. Inside of a month he followed me through the dooryard, woodyard, and garden much like a dog, although he was a very awkward walker, probably having had less use for his feet in walking than in carrying and holding prey. There were times when birds of his kind, often his mate without doubt, swept low above us. Then he would beat his wings and try frantically to fly. Sometimes he followed them with his despairing eyes as they sailed from sight, and sent after them a scream that never failed to set my heart aching. At such times I could scarcely forgive my father for having deprived such a royal bird of his high estate. Although he never said so, I believe from after events that my father had the same feeling.

By this time I had become known in the family as the unfailing friend of the birds. Every unfortunate bird caught in a reaper, wounded by having been stepped on by stock, or that had escaped from the attack of a cat, a red squirrel, or a snake, was brought to me for treatment. No one told me how to care for them. I was so intimate with each different kind that when a member of any bird family was brought to me I tried to do for it what seemed to be the right thing for a bird of its species. I think that in doctoring them I copied very closely the methods of my mother in treating our hurts.

CHAPTER II - A GIFT OF THE BIRDS

THE following year, one morning in early spring, my father called me to him to ask whether I should like to have as a gift the most beautiful thing ever made by man. Of course I eagerly assured him that I should like it very much indeed. Then he told me that he had something for me even finer and more precious than anything man ever had made or ever could make: a gift straight from the hands of the Creator. He then proceeded formally to present me with the personal and indisputable ownership of each bird of every description that made its home on his land. Undoubtedly the completeness of this gift was influenced by his experience with the hawk. Before that time if he had been making such a gift I think he undoubtedly would have reserved the right to exterminate the hawks that preyed on the fields and poultry, the owls that infested the barns and chicken houses, and very probably, too, the woodpeckers, which seemed to take even more of the cherries than did the robins, orioles, or tanagers. That he made the gift complete, with no reservations, proved that he had learned to regard my regard for the laws of nature, which, even when very young, I seemed dimly to realize and stoutly to maintain; for the worst hawk or owl was quite as dear to me and fully as interesting as the most exquisitely colored and ecstatic singer. He must have realized that the gift would not be perfect to me if there were exemptions, so he gave me for my very own not only the birds of free, wild flight with flaming color and thrilling song, with nests of wonder, jewels of eggs, and queer little babies, but also the high flying, wide winged denizens of the big woods, which homed in hollow trees and on large branches, far removed from any personal contact I might ever hope to have with them.

Such is the natural greed of human nature that even while he was talking to me I was making a flashing mental inventory of my property, for now I owned the hummingbirds, dressed in green satin with ruby jewels on their throats; the plucky little brown wren that sang by the hour to his mate from the top of the pump, even in a hard rain; the green warbler, nesting in a magnificent specimen of wild sweetbriar beside the back porch; and the song sparrow in the ground cedar beside the fence. The bluebirds, with their breasts of earth's brown and their backs of Heaven's deepest blue; the robin, the rain song of which my father loved more than the notes of any other bird, belonged to me. The flaming cardinal and his Quaker mate, keeping house on a flat limb within ten feet of our front door, were mine; and every bird of the black silk throng that lived in the top branches of four big evergreens in front of our home was mine. The oriole, spilling notes of molten sweetness, as it shot like a ray of detached sunshine to its nest in the

9

chestnut tree across the road was mine; while down beside the north creek, on a top branch of a willow sheltering an immense bed of blue calamus, nested a blood-red tanager, with black velvet wings. Every person visiting our family was taken to see him. With what pride I contemplated my next personally conducted trip to that tree to show the bird of blood-red! Now I owned the pewees in their marvelous little nest under the pig-pen roof, the song sparrow and the indigo finches of the privet bush at the foot of the garden, the swifts of our living room chimney, the swallows on the barn rafters, and the martins under the eaves. When it came to the orchard with its fruit trees and its shrub-filled snake fence corners of bloom and berries, I could not even begin to enumerate the vireos and bluebirds, the catbirds, robins, jays, and thrushes. Mine, too, was the friendly, delicately colored cuckoo, slipping through the shrub-filled fence corners and bushes of the woods pasture, with his never failing prediction of rain. I remember that in the first moment of tumultuous joy, one thought was to hope that a storm would come soon so that I might remark in careless, proprietary tones: "Hear my cuckoo calling for rain!"

In my enumeration, I included the queer little stilt-legged killdeer that had a nest on the creek bank of the meadow. I was on terms of such intimacy with her during the last few days of her brooding that she would take food from my fingers and even allow me to stroke her wing. There was another pair of hawks nesting in the big oak overhanging the brook a short distance farther in its course to the south; while I was as proud to possess the owls, from every little brown screecher in a hollow apple tree of the orchard to the great horned hooter of the big woods, as I was the finest song and game birds. In the greed of my small soul I saw myself ordering my brothers and sisters never again to take the eggs from any quail nest of the fence corners. I do not recall that I made a virtuous resolve at that minute not to take any more myself, but I do remember that the next time I found a nest of eggs it occurred to me that if I left them to hatch I should have that many more birds, so I never robbed another nest. In that hour I was almost dazed with the wonder and the marvel of my gift, and to-day, after a lifetime of experience among the birds, this gift seems even more wonderful than it did then.

That same day the search began for new treasures. No queen on her throne, I am sure, ever felt so rich or so proud as the little girl who owned every bird on her father's land. Ever since I could remember I had loved, to the best of my ability, protected, and doctored the birds, but I never before had realized that they were quite so wonderful. From that hour in which they became my personal property every bird of them took on new beauty of coloring, new grace in flight, and previously unnoted sweetness of song. So with the natural acquisitiveness of human nature I began a systematic search to increase my possessions. I climbed every tree in the dooryard and looked over the branches carefully. Not a sweet scented shrub, a honeysuckle, a lilac, a syringe, a rose bush, or a savin escaped my exploring eyes. Then I proceeded to the garden, and one by one I searched the currant, gooseberry, blackberry, and raspberry bushes, the grape arbor, the vines clambering over the fence, and the trees and shrubs of its corners. Then I went over each vine-covered section of the fence enclosing the dooryard, hunting for nests set flat on the crosspieces. I almost tore the hair from my head, while I did tear my apron to pieces and scratched my face, hands, and feet to bleeding in my minute exploration of the big berry patch east of the dooryard, where the Lawton blackberries grew high above my head. Then I extended my search to every corner of the fence enclosing the orchard and took its dozens of trees one at a time, climbing those that I could and standing motionless under those that I could not, intently watching until I am sure that few, if any, nests were overlooked. After that I gave the buggy-shed, the corn cribs, the pigpens, and the barn a careful examination and then followed the lane fences to the woods pasture in one direction and to the woods in the other. Lastly, I went with my brothers to the fields, and while they cultivated the crops, I searched the enclosing snake fences, with their corner triangles of green, filled with bushes and trees. It is my firm conviction that at that time there were, at the most conservative estimate, fifteen birds to every one that can be located in an equally propitious place and the same amount of territory to-day. Before I had finished my inventory I had so many nests that it was manifestly impossible for me to visit all of them in a day; so I selected sixty of those, which were most conveniently located and belonged to the rarest and most beautiful birds, giving them undivided attention and contenting myself with being able to point out, describe, and boast about the remainder.

As always ownership brought its cares. At once an unusual sense of watchfulness developed. No landholder was ever more eager to add to his acres than I was to increase my flock of birds. My first act was to beg my mother for an old teaspoon that I might have to keep. A green warbler in the gooseberry bushes, when stepping into her nest, had pierced the shell of an egg with the sharp nail of one of her toes. If the broken egg began to leak, it would stick to and soil the others and the nest. I was afraid to put my fingers into the small hair-lined cup, so I secured the spoon for this purpose and afterward always carried it in my apron pocket.

Life became one round of battles with cats, snakes, and red squirrels, while crows and jays were not to be trusted near the nests and the young of other birds. It was a long, tedious task to make friends with the builders of each of the chosen nests, for I was forced to approach very slowly and with extreme caution, imitating the call note of the bird the best I could; and when I had gone so near a nest that the brooding mother began to plaster her feathers flat to her body, to draw up her wings, the light of fear began to shine in her beady eyes, and she started to rise to her feet, it was time for me to pause until she regained her confidence and again settled to brooding. Almost always at this point a few more steps could be taken. I usually contented myself with leaving a little of the food that the bird being approached liked best to eat. On going back the following day, it would be possible to advance with confidence as far as I had gone the day before; from there on I would be forced again to work my way slowly and cautiously toward the nest. In this manner gradually the confidence of the mothers could be won so completely that it was permissible to touch them while they brooded. Some of the friendliest would look at me steadily for a long time and then, with a dart so quick that I had to watch myself lest I shrink back and frighten them, they would snatch the worm or berry held before them.

At that time I sincerely thought that it was my work to help those birds feed their young. Half of my breakfast slipped into my apron pockets, while I worked like the proverbial beaver searching the bushes for bugs, hunting worms on the cabbages in the garden, digging them from the earth, and gathering berries and soft fruits. I carried with me grain from the bins in the barns, pounded fine with the hammer and soaked until it was soft for the young of the grain and seed eaters. Few mothers were so careful about the food they fed their children. I gave those nestlings only one bite at a time, and never a morsel of anything until I had watched what it was that the old birds were giving them. Before the nesting season was over they allowed me to take the most wonderful liberties with them. Warblers, Phoebes, sparrows, and finches swarmed all over me, perching indiscriminately on my head, shoulders, and hands, while I stood beside their nests, feeding their young.

When it was decided that I had reached a suitable age to attend a city school, I stoutly rebelled, capitulating only when Father said the most precious of my birds might go with me. These, of course, were unfortunates that had fallen from their nests in high trees, where I could not replace them, those orphaned by an accident or some prowling creature, while sometimes a nest of young birds was brought me by a neighbour who thought he was doing me a kindness; so I left the country in company with nine birds, none smaller than a grosbeak, that had been raised by hand. I had to arrange my school day so that there was a morning hour in which to clean the cages, change sand, scrape perches, scour bath-tubs, and cook food.

My especial favorite among my pets was a brown thrasher named Peter, because he had constantly called: "Pe-ter, Pe-ter" in the distressful days when he was missing his mother and growing accustomed to my longer intervals between feedings. One of my brothers had found him helpless and dying beside a country road and had picked him up and put him in his pocket for me. When he was given into my care, he was half-starved. After a few minutes, he opened his bill for food, and in a short time spent in getting acquainted we became the greatest friends. He grew to be a strong, fine, male bird, and in the spring of his second year developed a remarkably sweet voice, with which he imitated the song of every bird that could be heard around our house. He also made excursions into improvisations, which I could not recognize as familiar bird notes. One warm night of summer my father suggested that Peter would be more comfortable if left on the veranda. That was a mistake. Either a screech owl or a rat attacked him in the night and broke the tip of one wing. In the morning Peter hopped from his open door and showed me his wing. We did all we could to comfort each other. I doctored him as in childhood I had doctored the hawk. I never shall forget the fortitude with which he bore the amputation, not struggling nor making the slightest effort to get away from me, although he cried pitifully. The wing soon healed, but Peter had lost his equilibrium. He never again could fly. Always before, he had had the freedom of the premises. Now he was forced to ride on my shoulder when I went out into the yard, or to hop after me. There was one particular apple tree of our dooryard in which there was a perch where I could learn a lesson much more easily than in school. While I studied, Peter hopped from branch to branch through the tree. One day under pressure of an especially difficult Latin translation I forgot to take Peter with me to the apple tree. A maid in the house saw that he was fretting to be with me, so she put him outside the door. I heard his call, realized he was coming, and climbed down as speedily as possible, but before I could reach him a prowling cat darted from under a shed and caught him. Powerless to give him any aid, I listened to his last, pitiful calls. With one exception he was the most interesting bird I ever raised by hand.

I still had left in my family a splendid cardinal that I think must surely have belonged to the bigger, brighter red birds of the West, a pair of our common Indiana cardinals, and a pair of rose-breasted grosbeaks with their family of four youngsters. The rose-breasted grosbeaks had built a nest in a tall maple tree growing between our sidewalk and the street. A night of high wind and driving rain broke from the tree the branch on which they had located and dropped it in our yard. From an upstairs window I noticed it early in the morning, my attention having been attracted by the distressing calls of the old birds. There was scarcely a trace of the nest to be found as it had been torn to pieces in the parting of the branches, but I did find every one of the four babies. They were too small for my ministrations, so I repaired the nest, put it in a cage, and set it beside the branch. In a short time the mother bird entered to feed the young. The door was held open with a long piece of string and as soon as she entered it closed. Then she was removed to a larger cage in the house. Inside of half an hour the father bird was captured in the same way. Then the cage was put in a partially darkened room with plenty of food and the parents allowed to take care of their young, which they did with scarcely a sign of protest. I was not particularly attached to this family. I merely helped them out of their predicament the best I knew how and when the young ones were old enough to become self-supporting all of them were given their freedom. During my last two years in school the work became so rigorous that I could not care for my pets and make a grade that would pass me, so reluctantly and not without many tears all of them were trained to become self-supporting and given their freedom.

CHAPTER III - BECOMING AN ILLUSTRATOR

AFTER three years of birdless estate I was so homesick for my former friends that I determined again to surround myself with a bevy of my favorite birds. Having established a home of my own one of the first considerations that came to me was how to fill the houses I still carried with me. The solution of my problem was under way when a niece of mine sent me a green linnet, produced by interbreeding with the canary tribe, a Harz mountain singer carefully trained. My first thought was to secure a mate for him. Through inquiry a neighbour was found who wanted to sell a hen canary having pure yellow color with white beak and feet, brilliant black eyes, not a discoverable feather off color. I immediately paid a rather exorbitant price for her and introduced her to my linnet. Theirs was a case of love at first sight. The nest was made by me from a collar box, a piece of white flannel, and some cotton padding. While the birds were busy with the affairs of housekeeping I had a house built for them at a factory in Cincinnati. It was six feet high, four long and three wide, the sides enameled white with gold decorations, and had a roof of moss green. This pair of birds accomplished three nestings their first season. The initial brood contained six sturdy youngsters, the second five, and the third four, so that I had seventeen birds for my new house at the end of the first summer. The young birds were of wonderful color, more than half of them sweet singers. Some of them were green like their father, some pure gold like their mother, some very largely gold with only a touch of green, while others had the green in predominance with beautiful markings of yellow; others had their color evenly divided between green and yellow, and two of the brood were a solid color of pure warm dusty tan, a shade I never before nor since saw produced in the feathering of a canary. Unfortunately both of these were hens.

With the last brood, in flying from her nest in haste, the mother bird dragged one of the young to the edge of the nest from which he fell to the gravel below. I found him in the morning and thought him dead. Picking him up I started toward the door to toss him out. While on the way a member of the family asked me a question so I stood for a few minutes talking. As I again turned toward the door there was a slight movement on the palm of my hand. I looked down to see that the tiny bare bird with his eyes not yet open was responding to warmth, so instead of throwing him away I returned him to the nest. Before the day was over he was lifting his head and taking food with the other young. When the brood left the nest I discovered that this bird had a leg out of joint at the socket. He could fly and hop around the cage as well as the others but the injured leg was longer, and while in use, it could be seen that the bird was a cripple. At once my family began to urge that the bird be removed from the cage and put out of what they termed "its misery." I watched the bird closely but could discover no sign that he was suffering any pain and only very slight inconvenience. In plumage, he was almost the clear yellow of his mother with a touch of green making a perfect cap jokily placed on his head at a very saucy angle, which gave him a particularly pert, ingratiating appearance. In size he was the largest bird of the brood and soon the largest in the cage. This may have been accounted for by the fact that he did not take as much exercise as the other birds, seldom leaving the top perch except for food or water, while when feeding he ate longer. Before any other of the young birds had begun to think of music, this one was trying to sing. In a year he had his father's whole repertoire, to which he added robin, song sparrow, and indigo finch notes that he learned from outdoor birds flocking over the conservatory, inside which his house stood. When he was two years old, with his feathers settled tight, his head tipped at an impertinent angle, his beak wide open, he lifted his voice above those of his brothers and father, and sang the most exquisite songs I ever heard from the throat of a canary. He had especial opportunities to learn music from a distant relative, the indigo finch whose nest was in a honeysuckle a few yards from the conservatory. This bird, from the top of a mulberry even closer, sang his full strain at the rate of five times a minute for an hour at a time several hours during a day, making by reliable mathematical calculation over two thousand daily renderings of his song for the greater part of a month. No wonder the canaries learned his notes the master singer especially. To me he was the dearest bird in the Cabin, while everyone admitted that he was the finest singer; but his broken leg was a daily annoyance to a member of my family. One day, during my absence, a woman, whose name and residence I could never learn, called at the Cabin begging to be sold a singer in order that she might raise young birds with a hen canary she had, and my best beloved bird was easily caught and given to her, which was a small heartbreak from which I never have recovered. When the birds of this cage were asleep in a row, filling the highest perch, with their heads tucked under their wings, and their feathers fluffed in cold weather, they looked exactly like gaudy swan's down powder puffs.

Shortly after this, a relative of my husband, who had been United States consul to Mexico, came home bringing me a wonderfully trained black-headed grosbeak which he had gotten from an Indian bird dealer in the market at Saltillo. This bird was black over the head and back, black on his wings and tail with touches of white, wearing a vest of warm, rotten apple brown. He was a magnificent singer, having sweeter notes than his rose-breasted cousin, and delivering them with more joyous spontaneity than the oriole. His call note was loud, clear, and sweet. He had an individual manner in rendering his stage performances which was as new to me as his person; for he was "a stranger in a strange land." He sang his full strain at the top of his voice. Then he dropped to a minor tone and sang exactly the same song, note for note; and then, with distended throat and beak so nearly closed that it could barely be seen to move, he gave the same performance pianissimo. Every note was given its full value but many times diminished to such mere threads and whispers of sound that I had to stand near him and listen intently to verify the notes. His strain was two or three times as long and much sweeter than that of his cousins the evening or rose-breasted grosbeak. As I did not know the history of his youth it appealed to me that he might have been taken from a nest when young and reared in the home of a professional bird-catcher, where he learned the notes that made up his repertoire from old birds of different kinds. This same bird dealer sold to the wife of the consul a gay assortment of exquisitely warbling little birds of blood-red, deep and pale blue, pink, yellow, rose, and purple. She released them in her conservatory with delight, but after their first bath they all proved to be pale yellow canaries gorgeously colored with Diamond Dyes, which were being introduced into Mexico at that time.

My grosbeak had a tender, loving disposition. He was always delighted to leave his cage and perch on my fingers or have the freedom of the room where the flowers were growing, but he was a shameless glutton. Undoubtedly he had been fed by hand when young and never had gotten over the habit, while his diet included almost everything. His gross beak proclaimed him a seed eater, but he flopped his wings and cried vociferously at the sight of fruit, berries, or vegetables, and almost "lost his head" over a luscious worm.

Every time I passed the cage he would spread his wings, open his mouth and cry for food like a nestling. He would fly from the perch to the floor of the cage and hop back and forth the length of it, begging for food while I was in sight. Because of this I formed the habit of finding, every time I went to the garden or among the outside flowers, a spider, a worm, or a juicy berry for him before I returned; so he grew to enormous size, having oily, glossy plumage, while he was almost a constant singer.

At about this time, a sister living in Michigan sent me a big African parrot. He was a gaudy creature, having a head and shoulders of the loveliest dark bronzy green. The extreme top of his head was pale blue and light yellow, his breast delicate light green, while his extended wings had feathers of blood-red, deep blue, yellow, and green. He was a fluent talker and a great musician, having been carefully trained to whistle a number of tunes that had been taught him with a flute. He was a fine addition to my bird family. When the grosbeak began to sing the canaries joined in; then the Major drowned all of them by his rendition in clear high notes of "The

Washington Post" march, which was a favorite performance; but, as in the case of the grosbeak, he could raise the notes high above the piano or flute and still keep them all of perfect tone, accurate measure and inflection, retaining pure sweetness.

That spring, merely to test his marksmanship, one of my neighbours severed the tiny twigs from which depended the nest of an oriole. In the long fall an unhatched egg and the youngest bird were destroyed, the two remaining seeming perfect and healthy. They were very young and required delicate attention and frequent feeding. I knew that in care of the woman of that family, the birds would be dead shortly; so I gave her a dollar for the little birds and undertook to raise them myself. When they were full grown I gave one of them to a friend, who seemed extremely eager to have it. The one that I kept had his living room in a big brass house, which was very attractive and of which he seemed to be extremely proud. The greater part of the day his door was open so he did as he pleased about remaining in his house. He was the bird I had in mind when I wrote previously that "with one exception" the brown thrasher was the best loved of all the birds I ever raised by hand. There is only one adjective that will adequately describe my oriole, and that is the much abused "charming." I always gave any bird I reared or accepted from a friend exquisite care. Their cages shone, their perches were clean, their baths were spotless, their food was freshly prepared every morning, they were given only as much as they would consume at a feeding, and the remainder was kept in the refrigerator until later in the day. All of my birds were larger and of richer plumage than those of their species in freedom.

My oriole had black parts of jetty blackness; his yellow plumage was a clear warm orange yellow; his eyes were like black diamonds; while, from having been brought up by hand and associated with me and daily receiving almost hourly attention, he had developed practically a reasoning, intelligent brain. He loved to fly around the room and perch on my head or shoulder. He liked to sleep on the back of my chair when I was sewing. He stuck his sharp, polished bill into almost every affair of my day. Very early in his career he began picking up any bit of thread or wrapping cord he could find in the conservatory or when he flew through the rooms, carrying these to his cage and spending hours weaving them back and forth between the wires. When I saw how busily he worked at this and how much pleasure he seemed to get from it. I gave him lengths of brightly colored woolen yarn and string to see what he would do with them.

One of the biggest fallacies ever published by any nature writer is the statement that male song birds do not work in the building of nests. The general rule is that they carry material assiduously, frequently entering the nest in the course of construction to try to help with the building. This the female almost always resents. I have watched the construction of a number of oriole nests from start to finish. With one in particular I spent three full days, so I know that half of the weaving and more than half of the material carrying was the work of the male. My oriole was particularly expert in weaving. One morning I cut pieces of loosely twisted coarse, stiff twine into lengths, pulling it apart and loosely rolling it into a ball about the size of a pint cup, and gave it to him to play with. He immediately stuck his head into the centre of the ball, worked out a hollow carefully, and began shaping around him the structure of an oriole's hammock for its nest exactly as the female bird weaves in freedom.

He loved water, often bathing two or three times during the day. He was a practical joker, one of his tricks being to pick up any large pebble from the sand in the bottom of his cage, carry it to the highest perch, and leaning over, drop it in his bath to make the water splash. So long as I watched him and laughed at him, he would keep this up. If I was reading and did not notice his performance, he would resort to some other means of attracting my attention. He was a fine musician and kept the house filled with joyous oriole notes all day.

In those days I was experiencing constant struggle to find an outlet for the tumult in my being. On a fourth of a square in a village not a mile from the Limberlost, we laid the foundations of a home. The lot was covered with several tall forest trees, an old orchard of eight apple trees, scattering peach, pear, plum, and cherry, and had been thickly planted years before with bushes, vines, and flowers. Here, my husband built the log cabin of my dreams for me. During my early days in that Cabin I went through more agony than should fall to the lot of the average seeker after a form of self-expression.

Because I dearly loved music I thought that might be my medium. Never was any one more mistaken, but I had to try several things before finding out what I had been born to do. While the musical fever endured I practiced for hours every day on the piano or violin. Soon I noticed when playing that the birds set up a perfect Babel of song. If the music was fast and loud, they sang in imitation. If my notes were soft and low, they warbled deep in distended throats. The parrot especially enjoyed whistling to the piano or violin but he disliked the song of the other birds and frequently broke off his most charming strain in order to scream harshly, "Shut up!" at the canaries. Having been taught to whistle with a flute the parrot soon became expert, while the other birds seemed to follow his lead. All of them did their best work with simple old melodies, played slowly. "The Carnival of Venice" seemed to be the most suitable, and the greatest favorite with all of them. After a long course of special training, feeling ready to perform before an audience, I grew vainglorious and wrote to my father to come and be convinced of the wonder I was performing.

Then one day my little daughter caught her apron on a nail and tore a long straight slit down it; so I drew the sewing machine from a closet and started to mend the garment. With the exception of the parrot, every one of my birds tuned up and sang "The Carnival of Venice" to the accompaniment of the sewing machine quite as well as they ever had sung with the violin or piano, so my concert never really materialized before an audience.

At this time I had also a pair of cardinals that had come around the house in a half-starved condition during a severe winter of unusual cold and deep snow, so that I enticed them inside in order to feed and take care of them. By spring they had grown so tame that I added them to my bird friends, but among all of them the oriole was my constant companion, my best loved bird. One day, forgetting that he was free, I stepped from a door and was slow about closing the screen behind me. A burst of jubilant notes above me first told me what I had done. I stood heartsick and watched my bird circle up and up, higher than I ever had seen any wild oriole fly. Then he slowly descended in curves and alighted on my head. I walked indoors, carrying him with me, but the mischief had been done. His exuberant joy in that short flight had been too apparent. From that day, I began training him to become self-supporting, and soon I gave him and the cardinals their freedom.

That same summer I lost the grosbeak through fatty degeneration. I discovered one morning that he was sick, and taking him from his cage for an examination, I was surprised at the size and weight of his body in my hand; while on blowing apart his feathers to discover the condition of his skin, I found that he resembled nothing so much as a small roll of clover butter. He died before the day was over, for no cause whatever except that he was so fat that he could not live. His was a marked case of having been "killed by kindness." Because he was a rare bird with us I sent his body to a taxidermist, who afterwards told me that the bird was so fat, his skin so thin and tender, he could mount it only by preparing a form and transferring to it little pieces not so large as his thumb nail at a time, so his work did not last long.

The more I studied and thought, the more clearly I saw, no matter how much I enjoyed having my home full of birds, I had no right to keep wild creatures in captivity; so I never replaced any of these birds. Long before I owned a camera or wrote a word on any nature subject my bird family was reduced to the parrot and canaries. I no longer needed to keep my home full of birds in order to enjoy all of the pleasure that might be had from them, for God had taught me that my gift endured, that all of the birds afield were mine, and that the only way to know and to study them rightly was as they lived, in the abandonment of perfect freedom.

Several years later I began writing on natural history subjects, and immediately the question of illustration arose. The editors who had accepted my work began to send me drawings of mounted birds, articulated with wire, stuffed with excelsior, and posed by men. It requires no great stretch of the imagination to understand how those pictures repelled me. I was horrified. Editors insisted upon illustration; I refused to allow the pictures they could provide to be incorporated in my text; so we were at a standstill.

The parrot solved my problem. He was an especial favorite with my husband, beside whose place at the dining table the bird frequently perched on the back of a low chair turned toward the table. In solemn and dignified silence the Major daintily ate food from a plate set before him. There were times when he grew tired of crackers and coffee, and saw something else on the table that he preferred. Then he would try to make us understand what he wanted. Once, after completely losing patience with our stupidity, he climbed from his chair to the table and with flattened feathers and in tremulous haste lest he be rebuked for this breach of discipline before he reached the object of his quest, he made his way among the dishes and snatched up a small green onion. Hurrying back to his chair he greedily ate three fourths of the hot vegetable. Several months later he displayed an unusual desire for something and we could not imagine what he wanted. Finally I suggested that it might be an oyster. He caught one from a fork and went hurrying back and forth across his chair, his wings half-lifted, fussing as he was accustomed to over something he had secured which he felt might be taken from him. He looked so comical that all of us laughed.

"Behold the antipodes!" I exclaimed. "Africa and Baltimore Bay! How I wish I had a camera!"

That was shortly before Christmas more than twenty years ago. A look not intended for me flashed across the table between my husband and daughter, but I saw it. Christmas brought me a small hand camera. Of course among the first pictures I attempted was one of the Major. That was a most amusing picture, sadly undertimed and overdeveloped; but before the weak streaky print left its first bath I was shouting through the Cabin like an insane creature, for although the picture contained almost every defect of a beginner's work I could see clearly that it was a perfectly natural, correct reproduction of a living bird. I had found my medium! I could illustrate what I wrote myself! I knew that with patient work the camera could soon be mastered in detail. How to make friends with the birds I knew better than any other one thing on earth.

Immediately I ordered a supply of chemicals from one of the leading drug houses of the country, laid in a heavy stock of print paper, and began work in the most intense earnestness. By spring I could make a technically perfect reproduction of the Major or any flower in the conservatory, while I even succeeded in photographing the fish in the aquarium, and, through the window glass, I made several really remarkable pictures of birds perching or feeding on the sills outside.

That spring, with the first dove of March, I went afield. I spent over a thousand dollars in equipment. All of the money accumulated from nature articles and a few stories went to pay for four cameras, each adapted to a different branch of outdoor work, also a small wagonload of field paraphernalia. I transformed the downstairs bathroom into a dark-room and used the kitchen sink for plate and print washing. These arrangements were extremely inconvenient and uncomfortable, as shutting out all light excluded air in summer and heat in winter; but I soon made prints which brought a prominent man of the Eastman Kodak Company to investigate my methods. He frankly admitted that their experts at the factory were not making as good prints on their paper as some I had sent them. I owned a Kodak, but as a rule all of my best negatives were on plates exposed in cameras. I did not subject the gentleman to the shock of showing him that my dark-room was the family bath, my washing tanks the turkey and meat platters in the kitchen sink. I first mastered the mechanism of my equipment, studied good works on photography and experimented with compounding chemicals and developing and fixing plates, and then the difficult processes of print making. At this time I was doing all of the work in the thirteen-room Cabin, except the washing, and was making most of the clothing worn by my daughter; so I was what might have been considered a busy person.

My first feeling on going afield was one of amazement at what my early days among the birds had taught me. Then I was merely amusing myself, following inborn tendencies. Now I learned with every approach to the home of a bird that I was using knowledge acquired in childhood. I knew what location each bird would choose for her nest, how she would build it, brood, and care for her young. When I wanted the picture of any particular bird I knew exactly where to search for its nest, so no time was wasted. When I found a nest, all that was necessary was to set up a camera before it, focus it sharply, cover the camera to the lens with a green cloth or a few twigs, then repeat the methods of childhood. The birds had not changed in the slightest; nor had I. By using tact, patience, and plain common sense, and drawing on former experience, in three days or less I was on a working basis with any nest of birds I ever attempted to cultivate, so that I could secure poses of the old birds performing every action of their lives anywhere in the locality of their nests.

I have reproduced birds in fear, anger, greed, pride, surprise, in full tide of song, while dressing their plumage, taking a sun bath, courting, brooding, and carrying food to their young. My procedure was merely to turn child's play into woman's work. My methods must be followed by any one who desires to accustom wild creatures to a state of fellowship with humanity. In order to do this it is necessary to move slowly, to live among the birds until one thoroughly understands their characteristics and habits, to remain near their locations until they have become s- accustomed to one as a part of their daily life that they will be perfectly natural in one's presence. The best friend I ever had in field work, Mr. Bob Black, an oilman operating leases beside the Wabash River, spent his spare time for several seasons locating nests for me. When I was extremely rushed, during the brooding months of May and June especially, by copying my methods he frequently trained families of birds for me so perfectly that they would endure my presence close enough to a nest to allow me to begin work with brooding pictures at the time of my first visit. He used a soap box set on stakes for a camera, his coat for a focusing cloth. With these he imitated my approach and work so closely that the birds paid no attention to me when I began operations.

Each student of bird life will rate the intelligence of the birds according to his ability to make friends with feathered creatures, to insinuate himself into their home life and to learn their secrets for himself. People who have not had much contact with them are the ones who insist that birds act solely upon instinct and are very wild. I have been upon terms of close intimacy with the home life of birds ever since I began to walk, and heretofore I have hesitated to put into print many of the experiences I have had with them, simply because the public is not yet educated to the point where it will credit my statements.

If I were compelled to pass an examination as to the number of bones in the bodies of my bird friends I should be in sad perplexity. I never have had the slightest desire or necessity to know so I do not intend to learn. If it became necessary for me to shoot one hundred and fifty rose-breasted grosbeaks in order to determine the number of potato bugs or of some certain "very tough worm," in their "little insides" then I should remain in ignorance as to the exact number they consume. On any point pertaining to the life, habits, and characteristics of the birds I can stand securely beside the doctors of ornithology, for few of them have had the incalculable advantage of beginning life with a gift of the birds, where birds homed in flocks.

CHAPTER IV - THE LURE OF FIELD WORK

TO THIS beginning I have now added more than twenty years of straight field work with every kind of camera on the market suitable for my purposes. In all this time the birds have been the main object of my search, but it would be impossible for any nature lover to spend this length of time afield, a large part of it being consumed in watching set cameras from some vantage point for hiding, without having accumulated a large fund of other experience. Upon many occasions I have had such rare and beautiful natural history subjects of other kinds literally thrust upon me that I have neglected the birds for their closest rivals, the moths and butterflies, while rare and exquisite flowers are always of intense interest to any field worker.

Aside from work I have done among the birds, I have photographed or painted in water colors every rare moth native to the Limberlost, as well as the common ones, and many of the most exquisite butterflies. The moth studies made the foundation for my book entitled "Moths of the Limberlost," while stray pictures of other insects, such as locusts, Katy-dids, dragon flies, crickets, and the like, combined with beautiful flower and landscape pictures, were the origin of another nature book, "Music of the Wild." I can truthfully say that with the exception of the months of May and June of one season, when I gave all of my time to moths, the real object of all field work I ever have done has been to bring from the deep forest, the woods pastures, the open fields, the swamps, meadows, orchards, and gardens, characteristic natural history reproductions of living birds. I have always reproduced each nest in its own environment exactly as the birds placed it, keeping the surroundings natural with the possible exception of tying back a branch here and there to allow sufficient light for pictures of action, such branches being released and restored to their former positions the moment the exposures were made. In securing thousands of negatives afield, I have resorted to every device my ingenuity could conjure up without the slightest regard to the amount of time, expense, or physical exertion that was required on my part. The one thing I never have done is to cut down a nest or in any way interfere with the home life of the birds, but gradually and with the greatest caution I have insinuated myself and my cameras into the birds' immediate surroundings.

One of the most interesting oriole pictures I ever made was taken by lashing two long, painter's ladders to one of the high telegraph poles of a city and fastening my camera on the opposite side of the pole slightly above the highest ladder; then by having a small boy climb the closest tree and tie back a branch, I could obtain a fine focus on the oriole's nest. For each picture I made in a long series I was compelled to climb those ladders to change the plates and reset the shutter.

On another occasion two men erected a platform for me level with the nest of a scarlet tanager, high among the branches of an extremely tall tree. The structure was so frail that it waved with every breath of wind and bent under my weight, but, as with the ladder, I was compelled to mount it in order to change plates every time I made an exposure with a long hose and bulb from a hidden location.

Sometimes I have worked in deep, dark woods where it was necessary to cut down a number of trees and bushes in order to obtain sufficient light for instantaneous exposure; again I have worked on embankments in the scorching suns of June and July without a trace of shelter. I have waded in swamps and braved the quicksands of lake shores, at times having mired until it was utterly impossible for me to extricate myself. I vividly recall one day at a lake near Silver Lake, in northern Indiana, when I entered the water shortly before nine o'clock in the morning and did not leave it until half past four in the afternoon, with the exception of a few minutes when eating a lunch at noon.

I have worked under bridges, in the unspeakable odors of vulture locations, near slaughter houses and crematories, in territory that was one shallow lake covering miles of surface in a June freshet; and once I worked under the rafters of an ice-house, where I had a fight to save my assistant from suffocation. He slipped from the top of the packed ice, on which we were setting up a camera, and fell eight feet below, between the side wall and the ice, the sawdust so covering and strangling him that he was almost helpless, while he could not gain a foothold either against the side of the building or the wall of ice. I finally got him out, while he was still able to help himself slightly, by taking a rail from a near-by fence, carrying it up the ladder by which we had entered a high door in the ice-house, and lowering it to him.

One of my very clear recollections of a choice day afield was in a swamp location of southern Michigan where there were so many big swamp rattlesnakes that my native guide, a temporary acquisition, refused to step from the conveyance, which carried us to the edge of the swamp; so I was forced to carry my tripods, ladder, and cameras and perform the day's work alone, or give up the pictures I had come to secure.

In all of these years of field work I have met with every peril that can be found afield in nature, to which there must be added tramps, vicious domestic animals, and cross dogs. I have braved the heat of the sun until my helper refused longer to work with me, and I have experienced the torture of chills, fever, and delirium from incipient sunstroke.

There is no way of gauging the hardships of a field worker. One of the most vivid recollections I have is of a day spent in securing two chapter tailpiece decorations for "The Song of the Cardinal." In the morning of a day of intense heat after a night of rain in late June, I almost suffocated in a steaming valley beside the Wabash River, where I was making pictures of a bed of wild morning glories; a few hours later, while wading the river to secure pictures of a bed of rose mallows, I contracted a chill which ended in congestion that gave me a ten day fight for my life.

There are hundreds of negatives in my closet, and if they could speak more than half of them could relate a thrilling tale of the hardship and dangers endured to secure them; but with it all I came through fifteen years without any broken bones and with no permanent damage done to my health except that after the near sunstroke I never again have been able to endure the same amount of intense heat for the same length of time as before. During the past five years, I have not been so fortunate.

One of the real discomforts of a professional field worker is the tiny red lice which infest many birds to such an extent it is marvelous that they survive. In handling the young of a shrike family, the history of which is given in a bird book of mine entitled "Friends in Feathers," I covered myself with these tormenting pests. Another day a friend who was helping me and I had the same experience with young quail from a nest near the Wabash; and later, on our farm, I had perhaps the choicest experience in this line. I was working on a nest of swallows under the floor of the upstairs of the barn, and in order to get the instantaneous exposure required to show the old birds feeding the young, I removed a large mirror from one of the dressing tables in the Cabin and set it up in the barnyard on a line with a window, so that it threw direct sunlight upon the nest for the greater part of an hour each forenoon. With the help of a ladder, I set up and focused my camera on the nest, waiting in a stall below for the appearance of the birds, climbing the ladder and changing the plates at each exposure. These birds were infested with red lice that dropped from the nest and fell from the old ones as they flew. Before I finished this series I made a practise of binding a napkin dipped in alcohol tightly over my hair, and at the finish of each hour's work I made a mad race for home, where I could secure a hot bath and a complete change of clothing. It is to me one of the marvels of nature that the tender young birds of a nest survive the myriads of red or grey or both kinds of bird lice which infest them. Sometimes they are killed by the large grey lice on the chicken feathers carried into nests for lining by the old birds.

I have gained a vast fund of experience in winning the confidence of birds and in reproducing their most intimate habits and characteristics during these twenty short years of field work with a camera. My negative closet now contains series after series made of the home life of birds, each nest reproduced where the birds located it, exactly as they built it, the birds being free wild creatures of the outdoors. Among the plates, now numbering thousands, I have a three months' series of the home life of a pair of black vultures, two months with a pair of kingfishers, and a complete pictorial history of the cardinal grosbeak. This last series includes a number of different birds, the collection extending over three or four years and comprising such exquisite and intimate pictures as a male bird in full tide of song, taking a bath in the rain, taking a sun bath, courting his mate, standing guard on the edge of his nest beside the brooding hen, and helping to feed the young, as well as the only picture I ever had the good fortune to secure of a hen bird working at the construction of her half-built nest.

For obvious reasons it is practically impossible to secure such a picture. To those who do not understand what I mean by this I offer the following explanation: all birds build their nests in what they suppose to be secure, sheltered locations. Very frequently they make mistakes, but with the shy, wild birds which I have pictured for the greater part, every nest location is chosen in the parting twigs, the crotch of a branch, or some place secluded and sheltered by leaves, roofs, rails, bridges, or embankments. The instant any mother bird at work on a nest feels that her location has been discovered she deserts that spot and begins a new one somewhere else. Always, in the work of nest building, she is in motion, either carrying material or weaving it into a cup, patterned around her breast, so that no picture of her is possible except through instantaneous exposure. To change the surroundings of a building female by the bending back of branches to let in sufficient light for instantaneous work would simply mean to drive the bird to the selection of a new location. She would not return to her first spot when a camera, however skillfully concealed, had been intruded, and brilliant sunlight was shining on the structure she had begun in deep shade.

I have made more or less complete series of the home life of the larger number of our shyest, wildest song birds of the interior. It is a far greater feat to secure a characteristic likeness of one of the song birds of deep wood or field than to point a camera at a flock of ocean or gulf birds and secure a thousand on a plate.

I have spent practically every summer of my life afield, more than twenty years of the time with cameras and other paraphernalia in active field work among the birds, work that required living from March to November in close, personal intimacy with them, and included the remainder of the year among the winter residents. Five years ago, through the work of farmers and lumbermen, my immediate territory had been cleared, drained, and put under cultivation, until the birds had flown, the flowers and moths were exterminated, there was not an interesting landscape left to reproduce. Then, in desperation, I haunted the state over, finally selecting another piece of true Limberlost country at the head of the same swamp region, where there are lakes by the score and miles upon miles of luxuriant swamp growth to attract the birds and perpetuate the flowers. Here, with the earnings from my work, I bought one hundred and twenty acres of rolling land, sloping abruptly to a small lovely lake, a mile of the winding shore line of which is included in my purchase. Also there are two fair-sized pieces of original timber, truly remarkable for the tall straightness of the trees and the wide range in variety; for I have chestnut oaks, blue ash, and coffee trees, as well as splendid red and white oaks, and grand grey old beeches, elms, lindens, and hackberries. Here, I practically reproduced the first Cabin, greatly enlarging it and adding a corner especially designed to facilitate my work; so I now have a library, dark-room, and a printing room, shut from the remainder of the Cabin, where I may work in seclusion. This I call Limberlost Cabin, north; the other, south.

I have had many unusual and unexplainable experiences afield. I have come to know the birds more intimately and to understand their ways better than those of my fellow men, with whom I have had no such contact. So if some of the happenings I record are not within the knowledge and experience of my readers I ask that before my veracity is questioned or an attempt is made to controvert the conclusions I draw, my lifetime of personal experience with the birds be taken into consideration, and that if I am to be questioned, the questioning be done by those who have had a like amount of similar experience. Naturally, I feel that having lived with and among the birds in such intimacy as to secure really characteristic pictures which exhibit the very human attributes of joy, grief, pain, fear, greed, suspicion, and the like, I should not be questioned except by those sufficiently intimate with the birds to have secured similar reproductions of them. I make no apology for any incident I introduce. In some cases I can offer incontrovertible proof by reliable witnesses, but very frequently my unsupported word must suffice, as of necessity in the more intimate and characteristic of these studies I have been obliged to go to the woods alone and to work with no disturbance whatever to the birds beyond my presence, which through days of intimacy they had been taught to ignore. Wherever it has been possible I have made photographic records to sustain my statements, but very frequently this was manifestly impossible because the subject was in motion in a place too dark or secluded for a snapshot, and some of the most wonderful things I record I have seen when passing through a wood alone, having no camera with me. Some of these happenings I have been able to verify by different birds of the same species, often enough that I have felt they might be attributed to the species as a characteristic; but most of the occurrences here described are isolated cases having been met with only once in my experience afield, so that nothing habitual or characteristic of an entire species could be adduced from such records; they are merely straws showing which way the wind blows.

CHAPTER V - UNUSUAL EXPERIENCES AFIELD

ONE day in searching along a wooded slope of the Wabash for birds' nests I noticed a small greyish brown bird fluttering among the leaves a few yards from me. I thought at first that she was practicing the subterfuge of the plover family and some of the other small game birds by pretending that she had a broken wing, in order to toll me from a nest location on the ground; but closer inspection disclosed that she was a female indigo finch in great distress. From her wide-spread wings and the manner in which she was gasping for breath, I imagined that her spine had been injured by a sling-shot or by something having fallen on her back.

On my going nearer she proved to be so nearly dead that she was unable to fly; so I picked her up to see if her trouble was apparent, and if there was any first aid that I could offer to an injured bird. I first examined her wings and found that they were not broken. Then I began blowing up the feathers on her back to see if there was a wound of any kind, but there was none. On reversing her to examine her breast and underparts, I was amazed to discover that her trouble was an egg so large that she could not deposit it. Then I knew exactly what to do because I once had a female canary in this same condition. I recalled also that on two occasions I had seen my mother operate on a hen for the same trouble. One end of the egg was exposed for perhaps one fourth of its surface. I took the small oil can from my paraphernalia and dropped a drop of oil on the exposed shell of the egg to soften the expanded parts as much as possible. Then, holding the bird firmly, I pierced the shell of the egg and broke it up with a hatpin so that it could be easily ejected. I then carried the bird down to the river and gave her water. In a few minutes, she was sufficiently recovered to perch on a small twig, and in less than five minutes she felt so much better that she flew away. I have no doubt that the next morning she began to deposit the remainder of her eggs in safety.

This is a thing that I have known to occur twice among birds and twice among poultry. Very frequently an egg is so large for a young hen in her first laying that it is deposited completely striped with her blood. Often, very large hen eggs prove to be double yolked. A few times I have seen a blood-stained egg in the nest of a bird, while almost without exception the first egg placed in a nest is noticeably larger than the others, and the last is smaller. I know, through years of experience, the nest of a young hen bird in the first building. A young hen can be recognized by her trim freshness and the fact that her plumage has not taken on the decided color of her species that comes after three or four moultings. Her location is not wisely chosen, her nest well shaped nor so compactly built as the work of birds having had experience. Such a bird having built such a nest, invariably produces a first egg very noticeably larger than the others.

Two other finch experiences are distinct in my memory. While working in the garden one May day, I noticed that somewhere nearby an indigo finch was in a frenzy of the mating song, and presently discovered him on the windowsill of the conservatory, hopping back and forth, his beak against the glass panes, trying to get inside, undoubtedly attracted by the foliage of a lemon tree, the flowers, and the song of his cousins in the canary house. This bird spent the greater part of one afternoon on the sill, until I was strongly tempted to open a ventilator and allow him to enter, but I could see nothing to be gained thereby, as he would only become alarmed and beat himself against the glass when he found he was confined in strange surroundings.

Late that evening a hen bird appeared, and the pair built a nest in a honeysuckle directly opposite the conservatory and perhaps thirty feet due west. There was an abundance of leaves and all sorts of nest material. I think that the female of this pair was a young bird. In the plethora of material and the exuberance of her first attempt, she built a nest twice the size of any of her kind I had examined in roadside, meadow, or thicket bushes, using copiously the dry last year's honeysuckle leaves, which she picked up on the ground under the bush. The size and peculiarity of this nest was one thing I wish to record. The other is the fact that the male appeared to be blind in one eye. Every forenoon about nine o'clock he entered the nest and brooded for an hour or more while his mate went to find her breakfast, bathe, and exercise. In setting up a camera before the nest in an attempt to secure such a rare picture as that of a male bird brooding, I noticed that he had flown against a thorn or some sharp projection, which had penetrated the inner corner of his right eye so that the ball was somewhat discolored and partially flooded, while a small red growth had formed in each corner. I thought that he was a bird several years of age, as his plumage was so fully matured through a number of moultings that when he brooded with the morning sun falling directly upon him, the top of his head and the feathers on the back of his neck were perfectly exquisite pale, greenish blue, shining like a highly polished gem of turquoise. I worked with this bird early in my outdoor experience, trying repeatedly to make him enter the nest and brood with his perfect eye toward the lens. For a number of mornings I tried to induce him to give me a study showing him in perfect condition, without at that time giving a thought to the fact that it might be extremely interesting to prove that the birds have accidents and sickness the same as human beings.

I always had noticed afield that after the construction of the nest had advanced for a day or two, each bird chose a separate route, by which to approach their location, and strictly adhered to that route in coming to the nest, leaving it by another and on the wing, wherever possible. This indigo bird had formed the habit of approaching his nest by flying to a certain twig of a bellflower apple tree near by, then to the pointed top of a board of the high alley fence, against which the honeysuckle climbed. From there, he would drop to the nest, every time bringing his bad eye on the side toward the lens. One morning I started to focus the camera on his location with my mind fully made up to saw the limb from the bellflower tree in an effort to make him seek a new route and approach from the other side; but when I reached the honeysuckle I found that the neighbor's cat had attacked the nest in the night, probably killing the mother bird – certainly tearing down the nest and eating the eggs.

The final intimate experience with an indigo bird came when driving from our farm one evening. I saw an abject spectacle in the shape of a bird hopping beside the road and climbed from the carriage to investigate. I knew by the bird's bill that it was a finch, but further than that I could not go in its identification as it had been completely immersed in crude oil, surrounding a well inside the fence. I took the miserable creature home, prepared a bath of Gold Dust in as hot water as the bird could bear, and with extreme care about the head and eyes, I tried to remove the oil. Only those who have had personal contact with crude oil can imagine what it meant to have the feathers of a bird soaked in it, then liberally sprinkled with the dust of the summer highway. I worked with all patience for the greater part of an hour, and nearly as long in cleansing the wash bowl afterward. I gave my bird a drink, some food, rolled him in a flannel cloth, and tucked him away for the night. His struggle in the oil had been too severe, too long endured, the bath too strenuous. In the morning I found that I had been working with an indigo finch, which was now extremely clean, also extremely dead.

For fifteen years all of my work was in oil country, which gave me the invaluable assistance of many oilmen in locating nests and working around them. I was at the same time in constant contact with crude oil, which is perhaps one of the nastiest things on earth upon footwear, clothing, and a working outfit, while in combination with a living bird I know of nothing worse. Ordinary soap will not faze it. In order to cut it, some especially strong compound like Dutch Cleanser, Snow Boy, or Gold Dust must be used with extremely hot water. The loss of the finch did not deter me from trying to save all of the birds I found in field work suffering from having fallen into oil or through having mistaken its glassy surface in some lights for water. The finch was the only oil-coated bird that died.

About the same time I had this experience, one of my friends among the oilmen brought me a much larger bird so plastered with dust and grease that I had no idea what it might be. The same methods I used on the finch brought this bird out the next morning, a lark fully grown, perfectly clean, but so utterly broken in spirit by his contact with the oil and his handling previous to and in the course of his cleansing that when I raised the flannel covering him, he crouched in the box like a young bird in a nest, opened his beak, and begged for food. I fed him the customary preparation of the yolk of egg made into a paste with equal parts of boiled potato and rolled hemp seed, freed as much as possible from the husk of the grain, and gave him water. After feeding him I lifted him to the edge of the box but he made not the slightest attempt to fly no matter how near any of us approached him. We even stroked his wings. I decided to try a daring experiment with him. I set up a camera, focused it upon an appropriate spot outdoors, carried him out as he perched on one of my fingers, cupping the other hand over him, and setting him on the spot, made almost a life-sized portrait of him. As he evinced no inclination to fly, I turned him in several positions; and finally, when I was ready to release him, he still showed not the slightest inclination to go.

At this time my daughter was closely associated with me in field work and it always had been her privilege to return to freedom all of the sick and the wounded that we had found or that had been brought to us for treatment; so when I finished every picture I could think of to make with the lark, I put him into Molly Cotton's hands that she might start him on his way to freedom. He sat there in perfect contentment until, at my suggestion, she shook him up a bit. Then he stood on his feet, but failed to fly. The Cabin, south, was located in a small village, immediately surrounded by fields, over which larks were constantly flying. Just at that point, one of his kind passed over our heads at no great height, singing the "Spring o' year" song of the lark. Instantly our bird found his voice, his wings, and his wild spirit. He uttered a sharp cry and flew at such speed that his going was merely an indistinct flash.

My worst experience with an oil-coated bird was that with a shitepoke, brought me by some boys who had found him while playing. I can not imagine what occurred to a bird with his length of leg and strength of wing to immerse him so completely in crude oil, unless from some high perch he saw an unfortunate small frog leap into a pool of oil, and like the frog mistaking it for water, he plunged also. Never before nor since have I seen a feathered creature make such an abject spectacle as did this oil-and-dirt-covered shitepoke, but my sympathies were so entirely with the bird that it never occurred to me to take his picture before giving him a bath. As was the case with the lark, he was so miserable and so cowed in his misery that he stood in the washbowl of my bathroom and allowed me to begin at his beak with a toothbrush and gradually move onward, cleaning every feather on him, and the skin as well, without making the least effort to get away; but when he was finished, thoroughly dry, and had rested over night, his broken spirit disappeared. He was ready to fly, also to fight for his freedom the instant he was uncovered in the morning.

There is nothing in an experience I once had with a pipit lark, except proof that birds are as subject to accident and injury as human beings. While I was driving one evening about six o'clock, a pipit lark on wing arose above a snake fence on one side of the highway, and crossed the road a few rods ahead of my carriage, dropping low as he flew. I thought he intended to pass between the rails of the fence he was headed toward and alight in a clover field. Whatever might have been his purpose, his estimate of space was wrong. Instead of passing between the rails, as birds do constantly in flight, he struck with full force, and fell on the grass of the wayside, lying motionless. I hurried to him, picked him up, and examined his beak to see that he had not broken it nor his neck. While I was handling him he began to revive and in a few minutes he was able to sit up, so I placed him on the top rail from which he very shortly flew to the clover field.

In writing of examining this bird's beak to see if it was broken, there comes to my mind the remembrance of a robin I once noticed in the dooryard in extreme distress. I was unable to capture this bird, but I could distinctly see that he had flown against something, squarely breaking off three fourths of the upper mandible, exposing his tongue, and incapacitating him either for pulling up angleworms, eating fruit, or taking a drink. He was crying pathetically. There is no question but he must have died very soon in much suffering.

While on the subject of robins, I might record my most unusual experience with these birds in having seen a white one in a flock, when they were massing for fall migration, congregating over some wild grapes on a country fence. This bird was robin in form, uttered robin notes, and was in robin country and company but had every feather on him of a soft dusty tan color, much like my canaries.

Among albino birds, in addition to the white robin, I once saw a robin with a large white spot on his shoulder, extending down one wing. The rest of his plumage was natural, so I figured that possibly this peculiar feathering might have resulted from a bruise, as I always have noticed that bruising or rubbing the hair from the skin of a domestic animal is very apt to result in the injured spot becoming covered by white hair.

I also have seen a large flock of English sparrows, of which two were a solid dusty cream color, and up to 1919 I have seen two white blackbirds.

I once worked with a pair of robins, one of whose young kept its head extended above the top of the nest, waving it and crying unceasingly, even immediately after the old bird had been to the nest with food. In the absence of the parents I climbed to the nest and discovered that the young one had been fed something of a poisonous nature, which had irritated its throat. A big water blister closed the entire food canal, while, the wind pipe

33

was badly crowded from the swelling in the neck. The bird could not shut its mouth, and could not swallow. I pricked the blisters, letting out the water, and tried the soothing influence of oil in the throat, but the bird died a few hours later in much distress. I wish now that I had taken the pains to see what its crop and gizzard contained. Undoubtedly its trouble arose from something it had been fed, as its entire body was full of inflammation, while at the same time it had slowly starved to death.

Another instance of extreme suffering was on the part of a robin I found in the orchard of our farm. Driving down the lane to the highway one evening at dusk, I noticed something unusual dangling from the branch of an apple tree, and heard pitiful robin calls of distress. I responded immediately and found a young bird so fully feathered that its condition seemed to indicate that it should have been several days from the nest, which gave no signs of having been occupied more recently. Being unable to reach the nest by means of the branch, which was too light to bear my weight, I went to the house to bring a ladder. As I approached the tree on my return, I found an old robin clinging to the side of the nest putting food into the mouth of the young one. When I reached the nest I discovered that this bird had a long, stout horsehair tightly looped around one of its legs just above the knee joint, both ends being firmly plastered in the mud of the nest foundation. It had hung by this hair for so long that the skin was cut to the muscle. The wound was so old that it had ceased to bleed, while the flesh had drawn back and was partially healed all around the cut, exposing the muscle, which was slowly being cut through by the struggles of the bird. I could draw no other conclusion than that this robin had hung there since it was old enough to leave the nest. During all this time the old ones must have fed it, as it was in fairly good flesh and its crop was well distended with food at the time I found it. All that was necessary in that instance was to break the hair and release the bird. I put it back in the nest, where it remained, as it seemed unable to stand on its hurt foot; but I hoped that after having been in an upright position for a time, it would regain its equilibrium and establish enough circulation to enable it again to use its foot.

At another time I saw a robin in our dooryard that had so nearly been the prey of a cat, red squirrel, or an owl that he had been forced to exercise a bird's prerogative and let his tail go to save his body. Farmers and people experienced in handling poultry know that a rooster or turkey, if grasped by the tail when pursued, can release the tail feathers to escape. I have noticed several instances and had my attention called to additional cases proving wild birds have the same power. This robin was full-grown, a bird of several seasons. I knew this by the ruddy color of his breast and the dark feathering of his back; but his tail, which was growing out again, was not more than three fourths of an inch in length and it could be seen that he missed it, for he attempted only short flights in which he seemed to experience constant difficulty, plunging forward, head down.

A very peculiar thing, which I have seen but once afield, occurred in a piece of swampy, low ground, filled with sturdy scrub oak, button bush, and low shrubs, where the presence of many birds proved it especially good nesting territory. Here one morning, on a dead limb in plain sight so that I could not possibly mistake my identification, sat a young blackbird squalling lustily for food. There were many blackbirds flying over him and feeding young of their kind in the bushes all around him, but not one of them gave this half-famished youngster a morsel. He evidently had left the nest only that morning, and I thought prematurely at that, for he had much difficulty in maintaining his balance on the limb. This may have been caused by his reaching toward every blackbird that passed him a widely yawning mouth, while he flopped his wings to attract their attention. This went on for so long that I decided his mother must have met her fate at the hands of a farmer, the crack of whose gun could be heard occasionally while he was planting corn in an adjoining field. Finally the young blackbird held his position with difficulty and seemed to be completely discouraged. A hen robin that had been carrying food to her young in a cottonwood in a line of flight directly over the blackbird evidently became as much exercised about the plight of the youngster as I was, for the next time she came with food she flew to the limb beside the blackbird and gave him a very generous feeding, which he seemed greatly pleased to take. This is the only incident of my life in which I have seen a bird of one species feed the young of another with the exception of small birds feeding cowbirds they had hatched in their own nests. The robin knew that all of her brood were intact in their nest in the cottonwood; she could only have deviated from her course and fed the young blackbird because he was a hungry youngster vociferously begging for food.

There are a number of wild cherry trees located very near Limberlost Cabin, north. When the fruit attains a juicy degree of ripeness and there has been a high wind during the night there are more cherries on the ground and these are more easily obtained for bird food than the fruit on the trees. Such a condition existed one morning in summer, as I was on my way downstairs to breakfast. I paused at a window at a turn in the stairs and looked into the west woods attracted by sounds of warfare among the birds. I was amazed to count seven pileated woodpeckers, four old and three young not long from the nest four red-headed woodpeckers, and four robins on the ground engaging in a battle royal over the cherries. This was the first time I ever had seen robins really fight with other birds. They seemed to be as pugnacious as the red-heads, which are stronger than they, and they seemed fearless in attacking the pileated woodpeckers, which are both larger and stronger. The battle raged the greater part of the day and it ceased entirely only when the ground was fairly well cleared of the fruit.

Probably from over two centuries of brooding near houses, robins have become tamer and more trustful of humanity than any other bird. Possibly there should be an exception in the case of the wren, but I am not sure; there are always three pairs of robins to one of wrens with us. They build where the logs cross at corners, under porch ceilings, and among the vines climbing on the verandas. Last year a robin built her nest on a windowsill directly against the sash of a summer residence belonging to my daughter. The nest was in a corner, its mud foundations so plastered to the sash that it was impossible to raise the window from the bottom until the young birds had flown, so the ventilation of the room was managed by the upper sash for the length of time the bird used the lower one, but as it was cool spring weather this worked no hardship for any one.

One of the most peculiar nesting locations I have encountered afield was on the running gear of a hay rake that had been left standing where the farmer had finished using it. The only protection that had been afforded it from the weather was the unscrewed seat turned upside down. On the crosspiece of the frame the bird had located her nest, so centred under the shelter of the overturned seat that it was perfectly protected from sun and rain.

A man in Richmond, Indiana, once sent me a photograph of a brooding robin. He wrote that the bird had been carried into the Union Depot of that city on the running gear of a freight car, having ridden on her nest, which the train crew said had been built in freight yards in New York City. The bird was the pet of the men about the yards, and much food from the dinner pails of the workmen was left near the nest for her convenience. The picture was certainly that of a live, brooding robin on the gear of a freight car, while the story seemed to be supported by ample and reliable proof, although it was in no way a personal experience of mine.

Heroic as the Richmond robin may have been, I have one robin experience which proves the bird of even greater devotion to her nest and young than that previously related. This robin arrived early and built in an apple tree outside the music-room window of the Cabin, south. The tree had been struggling with a bad case of scale for several years and had succumbed the past winter. The bird built in all confidence nearly fifteen feet from the ground at the branching of two large limbs, but not one leaf opened to shelter her from alternate driving spring rains and hot sunshine, as she surely expected. One day she baked in the sun; the following, she chilled in a flurry of snow. How she breasted one flood rain always has been a marvel to me. The tree stood on sloping ground outside a French window. Taking into account two feet of foundation and the slope, the nest was almost level with the face of a person standing inside the window. The

36

rainfall began on Monday morning quite early. From that time until ten o'clock on Thursday there was not an hour of daylight during which there was not rain heavy enough to keep the bird on her nest to shelter it and her eggs. Much of the time there was a deluge that forced her to stick her beak straight up and gasp for breath. During daylight some member of the household was almost constantly on watch. Never once did the bird leave her nest or the male bird bring her food or relieve her long siege of brooding. It rained and it rained, until I thought that the mud plastering of the nest foundations would dissolve so that it would wash away from under her, but she had built an unusually large nest with much grass and straw covering the outside of the body so that it endured. I thought that she would become so wet that the water would run down her body through her feathers and chill the eggs until they would be spoiled. In the heaviest of the downpour I truly thought that the bird would drown on her nest or die from hunger. We seriously discussed trying to wire an old umbrella over her or fixing a box above the nest but any shelter we could arrange before her eggs quickened to bind her to them would drive her from them so long that they would be chilled. So we watched, marveled, but did nothing. At ten o'clock Thursday the rain ceased, the clouds scattered, the sun shone. From the length of time the robin had remained in the same position during all of those hours of cold drenching and hunger, she staggered when she finally arose in her nest, uttered the robin tribal call, and attempted flight. I was watching, s- I saw her miss the branch of a near-by plum tree and fall among the bushes below. There she gained a footing, rested awhile, and then flew to the branch she had first started toward. After another rest she wavered to earth and ate angleworms until my next fear for her was that she would burst. While she was feeding her mate flew down to her and they talked over the situation. I certainly should have been interested in knowing exactly what she said to him. He flew to the edge of the nest and carefully inspected it and the eggs, but even then he did not enter it to brood awhile for her. The mother bird soon went back to her nest. She left it more frequently than usual the remainder of that day, but the following day she seemed to have recovered from her rough experience. Three eggs of that nest hatched, so that only one bird was lost and I have no proof that it failed to develop on account of the storm. That mother robin stands monumental to me as the most heroic of the birds of my personal experience. I am convinced that she brooded under the conditions described without having once left her nest from the time she entered it for night, about four o'clock Sunday afternoon, until ten o'clock Thursday morning – ninety hours. This experience clearly proves that human mothers are not the only ones who make sacrifices for their young.

CHAPTER VI - UNUSUAL EXPERIENCES AFIELD

ONE spring morning, after the owls had raised pandemonium in the night in the wild grape vines surrounding the spring at the Cabin, north, when passing along the path leading to my east woods I found under a small wild crab tree heavily loaded with bittersweet vines most of the tail feathers of a cardinal grosbeak; and a few yards farther along, the remainder. Later in the day, I saw the cardinal without a vestige of tail. He was experiencing even greater difficulty in flight than had the tailless robin. He could fly in stretches of a few yards, but he did not seem to be able to keep his head up and guide his course in the usual manner.

A woman in the southern part of the state wrote a few years ago to tell me that for the greater part of one winter a male cardinal roosted under the eaves near a kitchen window on a vine climbing the side of her residence. One night during the winter he had perched in such a manner that his tail touched a water spout running horizontally from the eaves to a turn at the corner of the house. During the forepart of the night water had dripped from the eaves, wetting his tail. As the night advanced and grew colder, ice formed, freezing the tail to the pipe. In the early morning when the woman looked to see if the bird was there she saw only his tail fast to the pipe. She had taken a step-ladder and secured the feathers. She wanted to know whether losing the tail would kill the bird, and she also stated in her letter that he did not again return to his former perching place.

I had another letter concerning a cardinal. This bird was reported to have visited a certain western window every afternoon about four o'clock and in repeated instances fought with his own reflection on the glass for an hour at a time. I had had this same experience in a limited degree. Three different times in one afternoon a blackbird put his bill against the glass of my bedroom window and tried repeatedly to walk through it, not seeming to understand why he could not. My bird did not seem to be pugnacious, merely inquisitive. The window was rather heavily covered with a wild rose bush, and the glass had only that morning been highly polished during the course of spring house-cleaning. At the third appearance of the bird I went outside to see what his view would mean to me. The late sun in travelling around to the west shone obliquely across the window, which faced due south, and what I saw where the bird had been appeared to me exactly like a pool of water surrounded by wild rose leaves; so I have no doubt that the bird from the same point got the same effect.

All one season a song sparrow having a broken wing lived in the honeysuckle of the blue finch and among the rose bushes, blackberries, raspberries, and wild roses of the west fence where it extended down to the garage beside the garden, at the Cabin, south. He could hop from the ground to the branches of the bushes and from there make his way higher even to the girder of the fence, from which it was possible to reach two different apple trees. By extending his sound wing and spreading his tail he could fly from the low branches of the apple trees to the ground without seriously hurting himself. I watched him with anxiety and always kept crumbs on the ground under the honeysuckle and in a secluded place on the fence girder. He was there throughout the summer and until very late in the fall, his chirp constantly sounding, but his spirit had broken with his wing, for I never heard him sing a note. When the leaves fell and he lost their shelter he was peculiarly exposed. Early in November he disappeared. I think very likely he was the victim of a prowling cat, as these birds or others exactly like them from farther north were with us all winter.

One morning as I was walking through the woods of our farm after a night of heavy rain my attention was attracted by the alarm cries of grosbeaks and scarlet tanagers, while from the ground I could hear the feeble cries of young in distress. I was not prepared for field work but I entered the swamp, balancing myself from hummock to hummock and walking on old logs and fallen branches, where a short search revealed one young grosbeak and one scarlet tanager. There remained traces of the grosbeak nest in a thicket of wild grape vines but I could not find the location of the tanager nest. The frail tree with the vines creeping over it was too light to bear my weight. To leave the young birds meant for them to flutter into the water or be trampled by cattle, which frequently made mad rushes through the vines to rid themselves of the torment of flies settling on their backs, so I carried the nestlings home in my hands.

That night I read in a work on ornithology that a young hawk taken from his nest of large sticks and coarse rough material and put in a soft nest would die miserably. The following morning I returned to the swamp with a ladder. There had been some woodland tragedy other than the storm. The grosbeak nest contained one baby, dead and badly abused, so I carefully cut away the surrounding vines and brought the cradle home to my birds. Then for ten days, in the midst of my busiest season afield, I stopped every fifteen minutes to feed those two youngsters a mixture of equal parts of boiled potato and hard boiled egg, varied by the addition of a little fruit, at times bread and milk or rolled hemp seed. When I was compelled to go afield, for a week or ten days, their nest placed in a small box and covered with a cloth was carried with me so that they might be fed regularly. Sometimes their field feedings were farther apart than those at home but at no time did they go longer than half an hour. They grew finely. When they were large enough to fly well they had the freedom of the conservatory. Then the door was left open and at last they were placed in an apple tree near the back door with their food and water convenient. It was not long until they could take care of themselves. For several weeks I could see them and hear their voices as they flew through the orchard. Then they wandered farther afield and finally deserted me altogether.

One of the greatest tragedies I have known of afield was revealed by the body of a Baltimore oriole hanging from a loop of cotton cord in a cottonwood, not far from a partially completed nest that evidently had been abandoned on account of the accident. In carrying material one of the pair had dropped a piece of cotton cord mixed with heavy sewing cotton. This had lodged on the stiff point of a dead twig, then had been worked back by the wind until it caught on a tiny projection of the twig made by a falling leaf. The male oriole in working to free this material in order to use it as a lashing to fasten his nest had slipped his head through a loop in the string, so fashioned that when he had pulled it to slip it off the twig it became a veritable noose, which grew tighter with his struggles until it had choked him to death.

As this oriole and the robin are the only examples I recall having seen of birds trapped in nest material, when almost every nest visited has hair, string, and plant fibre in which they easily could entangle their heads or feet, I deem these isolated cases excellent proof that the birds are extremely deft in the business of building; and it is one of the rarest experiences of the woods to find a bird in difficulty through its awkwardness in handling its building material.

The nest of a scarlet tanager is a beautifully built structure, placed, in comparison with the average locations of other birds, at extreme heights. I have not examined many of them, but all I ever have seen at close range or observed through glasses were neat and clean, giving every evidence that the old birds emptied the cloacae and carried away the excrement, as is almost the universal rule. In climbing to the heights of a tanager nest one day to make a record of the state of its progress, one of my field assistants reported to me that one of the nestlings, perhaps four or five days from the shell, was in serious trouble which he thought I might relieve; so I told him to slip his fingers under the feet of the little bird so that it would not cling to and tear up the bottom of the nest, put it in his pocket, and bring it down with him. When he placed it in my hands I found that the top of its head, both of its eyes and its nose were thickly plastered with a deep coat of excrement, to which the down of the other nestlings and the fine feathering of the mother bird had adhered until it was blinded. Having no conveniences with me with which to operate on such a case I carried the young bird home, warmed some milk, dipped a cloth into it, and bound it over the top of its head until I had soaked loose all foreign substance. Its eyes and the entire region surrounding them were the palest of coral pink. It seemed at first as if the bird would be permanently blind. I put it in the dark, fed it for a day or two, gradually introducing light, and by the end of the second day its eyes had returned to almost normal color, while a number of experiments convinced me that it could see as well as any young bird. It was then returned to the nest, from which the rest of its family had not yet taken wing.

I have had trouble with a window on the front porch of each Cabin on which the surrounding trees throw green reflections, while the glass takes on the lights of water. Several times birds have been deceived by this and in striking the glass in flight have either killed or severely injured themselves. One of the first instances of this kind was that of a ruby-throated hummingbird that was knocked limp and helpless, but soon after being picked up he revived sufficiently to fly.

Very late in the fall I once found on my front porch the dead body of a ruby-crowned kinglet, a tiny pinch of bone, muscle, and delicately colored feathers, with a little dab of red on the crest. The bird was the first of the kind I ever had had in my hands, as kinglets live farther north and come to my locality only as winter migrants. Because he was so rare and so beautiful I sent this bird to a firm of taxidermists, considered reliable; but when I called for my bird no one knew anything about him. I took the pains to trace the firm's signature for the receipt of the package containing him, on the books of the express company, but still they insisted that they had not seen him. Undoubtedly some collector paid them far more for his mounted body than they would have dared ask me for doing the work, since they would scarcely have signed for an express package and failed to open it.

The largest bird that I ever found dead from striking the glass was a woodcock. Between these extremes, perhaps half a dozen other birds have lost their lives on these windows, while repeatedly there is evidence on the glass that it has been struck by some bird in flight, injured so slightly that it has soon flown away.

While about my work in the oil fields one morning I was told by one of the oilmen that a neighboring farmer had just shot a hawk for carrying away young chickens. The oilman knew the location of the nest and thought the bird killed was the female. We went to the spot. He climbed the tree and found one egg in the nest, which he carefully brought to the ground. We put it in the nest of a hen that was brooding in a tool-house. I considered it a scurvy trick to ask a patient, law-abiding hen to brood on the egg of her worst enemy, but the egg had become so chilled during the length of time it had been uncovered that it never hatched.

I have had two very intimate experiences with hummingbirds. On the streets of our village one morning a man who always made an effort to help me about my work held his hands cupped together before me, saying after the manner of the old game: "Hold fast all I give you." What he gave me was the body of a ruby throat. I thought at first that it was dead, that he had brought it so that I might make a minute examination of its plumage and anatomy or have its body mounted. Before I reached the Cabin it showed signs of life, so I put a drop of brandy into a few drops of water, added a few grains of sugar and gave it a drink. The time was late fall and there had been a heavy frost the previous night. For some reason this bird had been slow about migrating so it was almost frozen to death. When I saw that it was reviving I carried it back of the Cabin, where I had covered a la France rose bush the night before in order to save the buds as long as possible. I set the bird on the rose bush and took its picture. Then I gave it another drink. It sat straighter and seemed to feel much better so I tried another pose. Then I administered another drink and put a fresh plate in the camera. By this time the bird had fluffed its feathers and settled its plumage, which had been somewhat ruffled through handling. As I reached for the bulb to make a third exposure the familiar hum of wings above my head told me that my subject had taken leave of me. As far as I could see the little creature, it headed its flight due south. I doubt that it made a prolonged stop until it reached Florida or Central America.

Perhaps my most puzzling experience with a hummingbird occurred when Molly Cotton gave her ice cream money to a boy as the purchase price of a hummingbird he had accidentally hit with a stone from his sling-shot. She brought the bird to me, demanding in all confidence that I doctor it. From the position in which it lay in her extended hand I thought its back was seriously injured if not broken. I had not the faintest idea how to render first aid to an injured hummingbird, nor could I fail the expectant eyes or disappoint the tone of conviction in my girl's voice when she so confidently demanded that I "do something." More in order to convince her that I was doing something than because I felt I could do anything effective I put the hummingbird into an empty nest in the conservatory, giving the little creature a drink of sweetened water. It drank as if it were famished, running its long, threadlike tongue over the bowl of the spoon, searching for particles of sugar. We then surrounded it with the bloom of honeysuckle and trumpet creeper. When the flowers were held within its reach it fed on the pollen and never refused the water.

I confidently expected that it would be dead the following morning, but instead it had folded its wings, which drooped the day before, and was clinging to one of the coarser twigs of the nest with its feet. At these signs of improvement I began to work in earnest. I removed the nest to a cool, shady place, and added to the bird's diet hard boiled egg, thinned almost to liquid and sweetened. By the third morning it could move its body and use its feet, for it had climbed to the edge of the nest. Both of us rejoiced, seeing that our bird was going to recover. I blame myself for the accident which followed. From the fact that the bird was strong enough to climb to the edge of the nest, I should have been warned that it would attempt to fly and placed it in a lower position. Shortly afterward, it tried to take wing,

42

falling from the shelf four or five feet to the cement floor of the conservatory, so aggravating its original injury that it soon died.

Perhaps my most unique experience with a bird occurred rather late one fall. On the way to the river one morning I noticed a bird acting peculiarly on a fine specimen of pokeberry. There had been a frost the night before. A hot autumn sun was shining on the frozen fruit. On going closer to see what was happening I found a cedar waxwing, a bird native to my location but for all that extremely rare, one seen less frequently than almost any other bird of my acquaintance. The waxwing was feasting continuously on the frozen berries, and almost as continuously raining them down in the form of scarcely digested excrement. He was in such a state of intoxication that he did not always secure the berry at which he aimed and the plumage of his face and throat was badly stained with the juice. He was so unsteady on his feet that he frequently lost his balance and plunging headfirst he fell to the underside of the little branches to which he clung with his feet; but hanging head down, and even while he was struggling to gain an upright position, he still continued eating every berry he could reach. Approaching as close as I thought I dared I exposed two or three plates, while my assistant hurried back to my base of supplies for more plates. I first began so far away that the picture included the whole bush, which was shaped like a small tree, having two or three trunks, then advanced gradually until my last plate was gone. When no longer able to take pictures I tried the experiment of seeing how close I could approach and found to my surprise that the bird was unable to fly. I could pick him up in my hands. He did not exhibit the least sign of fear, so I put him back on the bush and left him in what could be considered nothing less than a state of intoxication, which I could have reproduced even more intimately than in the pictures I had secured if I had known that he was past flight before using my last plate.

Previously, I had one experience with wild creatures becoming intoxicated, when, in order to get more light on my subject, Mr. Black trimmed the lower branches of a young crab tree while the sap was still running. The liquid quickly fermented in the hot spring sunshine. Soon the trunk was covered with butterflies, moths, bees, ants, and flies, all of them becoming rapidly intoxicated. This occurrence happened early in my field work with a camera and was both pictured and described in my first nature story. I have frequently been told that our robins and other Northern birds become intoxicated on fermenting fruit and berries during their stay in the South, getting themselves into such a soiled and repulsive condition that people have small compunction about shooting them to reduce their numbers.

During my experiences afield I have met with several instances of isolated birds not supposed to belong to my territory. Early in my work afield with a camera beside the Wabash River and confined to the same stretch of territory for two seasons, I heard the notes and frequently saw the high-flying form of a lark, which could have been nothing but an English skylark. I called upon my undefended head the harsh criticism of a number of writers on ornithological subjects by describing the high flight of this bird and his exquisite song among the clouds, when he seemed literally to soar to the gates of Heaven. As I recall, I described him as flying higher than any other bird which sang on wing, and this is exactly what he did. I never succeeded in getting sufficiently close to him to differentiate his markings and feathering from our meadow larks which were constantly singing from rod lines, high fence posts, and other points of vantage about as high as the average tree, or singing on wing, but in flight not so high as the goldfinch or oriole. Just at the time when I was most severely criticized for describing this lark of high flight and exquisite song, the facts were made public in the newspapers of the East that several men had some British skylarks captured, brought to this country and released in an effort to add them to our ornithology. I am sorry that I lost this clipping and can no longer give its origin, for undoubtedly it was a skylark from these importations, which for two seasons sang above the Limberlost. The reference to bird importations in the West met a better fate and can be quoted in its entirely. Mr. C. F. Pfluger, Secretary of the Association for the Importation of Songbirds into Oregon, makes the following report:

In the month of May, 1889, the society imported from Clausthal, in Germany, under a contract with a German bird-dealer, the following birds in pairs of males and females, viz.: ten pairs of black-headed nightingales, eight pairs of gray song thrushes, fifteen pairs of black song thrushes, twenty-two pairs of skylarks, four pairs of singing quail, twenty pairs of black starlings, nineteen bullfinches, three of which were females and sixteen males (the rest of the females had died on the way), forty pairs of chaffinches, thirty-five pairs of linnets, forty pairs of ziskins (green finches), twenty pairs of cross-beaks, one pair of real nightingales (the rest had died on the way), and several pairs of red-breasted English robins, the European wren species, forest finches, yellow-hammers, green finches.

When these birds arrived here, each species was put into a large wooden cage six feet high, six feet long, and four feet deep, with wire-net front, with plenty of water and their favorite food, thus giving them a good opportunity to rest and exercise their wings before they were turned loose. All these birds, with their cages, were placed on exhibition for four days to the public. Thousands of people went to see them, and the society realized about five hundred dollars by this show, which went toward paying for the expense of bringing them here. At the close of the exhibition the birds were turned loose under direction of Frank Dekum, president of the society, in the suburbs of Portland and in other counties here.

The larks were let loose outside of the city near clover meadows.

The birds have done well ever since they were let loose; we watched them all through the summer of 1889. Some nested in Portland and some in the suburbs, while others went far off into the State.

We have had very flattering reports of these birds from all parts of the State.

The birds left here in the fall of 1889 and returned in the spring of 1890, except the black thrush and the skylark; they did not migrate.

The society has received reports from numerous places in this vicinity which show that the birds brought here and turned loose a year ago last spring, have prospered, and that the scheme has been a grand success.

These birds did so well that the same society ordered for March, 1891, through a Portland bird-dealer named Stuhr:

Twenty-four pairs of skylarks at $4 per pair, twenty-four pairs of American mocking-birds at $5.50 per pair, twenty-four pairs of bullfinches at $4 per pair, twelve pairs of black song thrushes at $7.50 per pair, twelve pairs of gray song thrushes at $8.50 per pair, eighteen pairs of red-breasted English robins at $5.50 per pair, twenty-four pairs of black-headed nightingales at $5.50 per pair. Some special orders for different parties were of goldfinches at $2.50 per pair, black starlings at $5.50 per pair, chaffinches at $2.50 per pair, linnets at $3.50 per pair, ziskins (green finches) at $2.50 per pair. The aforesaid birds have to be delivered here in first-class order and healthy condition by Mr. Stuhr, the bird-dealer, and upon such delivery he will be paid for the same at the aforesaid prices.

This is a move in a most interesting direction. Why should we not have nightingales, bullfinches, linnets, and larks, if they can be bought so cheaply and will acclimatize and be happy with us? Near this time, Mr. Bok wrote me concerning the feasibility of releasing some European nightingales on his residence grounds at Merion, Montgomery County, Pennsylvania. I advised Mr. Bok and two other men, who asked the same question, by all means to try acclimating the nightingales and larks also. There is no reason why we should not add exquisite singers to our ornithology as well as rare orchids and other imported flowers, shrubs, vines, and trees to our horticulture.

In the case of two other strange birds, I have no hesitation in saying: "I know." One day while working with a guide in an open piece of woods pasture with clumps of thickly growing trees while we crouched motionless in hiding waiting for a pair of rose-breasted grosbeaks to come to their nest on which I had two set cameras focused, there burst on our ears such a bedlam of song that we were fairly dazed. The time was about half past three in the afternoon. I thought at first that the notes were those of the brown thrasher, but presently I discovered that this bird was singing as no thrasher ever sang. He was imitating the bold, clear notes of the lark, and every song that lay between that and the tiniest wisps of sound made by a gnat-catcher or hummingbird; and when he interrupted this performance to imitate the crowing of a rooster, the bark of a dog, the rattle of a hay wagon on the highway, and the neigh of a horse in an adjoining field, we came from hiding, cautiously crept through the willows and underbrush until we could get a clear view of the singer, perched in the tiptop of the highest poplar tree of a clump nearby, singing to split his throat. He was a bird of pure greys with a greyish white vest and touches of white on his dark wing feathers. There is nothing he possibly could have been except a Southern mocking bird. I was extremely familiar with three birds of this kind, which were kept in captivity at that time in a home of a friend of mine whose residence lay scarcely a mile away on the outskirts of the village. I was so sure that one of his birds had escaped that I stopped at night on my way home to tell him where his pet could be found, and to make sure again that I could not be mistaken in the identity of the singer. The birds were all in their room. They were exact reproductions of the one I had heard. Returning to work the following morning in the same location, I took with me my daughter, who recently had been visiting in Asheville, North Carolina, where, I had heard her say, these birds were very numerous and almost impudently tame. I did not tell her of my experience the day before, but took her with me to the blind where I had been hiding, fervently hoping that the mocking bird would be in the same locality and sing again. About ten o'clock I heard him calling in the bushes, and a few minutes later he began to sing. Then I led her where she could see him and asked her what he was. She promptly answered that he was a mocking bird, so I had her corroboration and that of my helper who knew the caged birds well. I worked throughout the summer, the greater part of the time in or near this location, but never saw or heard the bird again. The ornithology of Indiana now includes this bird in the southern part of the state, while it is listed as a stray even as far north as the southern part of Michigan.

The other incident, concerning which I know I shall be questioned but in which I also know I am right, occurred about fifteen years ago, while I was in field work with a camera. I was hiding in a fence corner on one side of a highway lying about a mile south and three miles west of the Limberlost. On the opposite side of the road I had a camera focused on the nest of a pair of birds in some bushes in a fence corner. While I was waiting for the birds to return from food hunting there was a whistling of wings, suggestive of wild doves or domestic pigeons, but much clearer and higher than anything I had heard since childhood. A bird alighted on the telephone wire almost directly opposite where I was hiding. It was as large as the largest domestic pigeon I ever had seen, longer and trimmer in shape, having a long tail of only a few feathers; its beak and feet were unusually red, as was its nose. Over the top of its head and shoulders there was a most exquisite metallic lustre of bronze, tempering to shifting shades of the same color only lighter on its breast. Its back was a slate grey with faint bronze lights, while here and there over its wings there was a tiny, dark feather. The bird was very alert, its head high-head, its big, liquid eyes searching the landscape in all directions. As it struck the wire it gave a queer cry – nothing like the notes of our doves or pigeons, but in a high key and interrogative tone it called as nearly as I can express it in words: "See, see, see." Then it searched the landscape all around it, called again not so loudly, listened intently, and again took up its course straight west. There was nothing this bird could have been except one of the very last of our wild pigeons. I had heard it described all of my life, had seen it in our woods in my childhood, and before this experience I had carefully studied the pair in confinement in the Cincinnati zoological gardens; so I know I was not mistaken in my identification.

Another extremely rare bird in my locality which I have seen only once in a flock in the woods of the Cabin, north, early in November, is the white snow bunting of the North, lightly touched with rusty red brown over its back and wings. It may be common with other field workers, but I have seen it in only this one instance.

To birds noticed in locations which were unusual for them I might add the loon. Early one spring while working beside the Wabash River I was amazed to see a loon swimming toward me. I examined him carefully to make sure of my identification, but there was no mistaking his pointed beak, white band around his throat, and his extreme agility in the water. I imagined that he had alighted flock in migration for a drink or to feed upon the bank. As I never had seen a loon in flight I tried to make him take wing, but he swam steadily with the current, all the time coming closer to me. At the wildest demonstration I could make he dived and very shortly came to the surface quite a distance below me. Then I took a straight cut across a bend in the river bank so that I should once more be in front of him. When he approached me the second time, from what I hoped was concealment, I threw a stick into the water directly in front of him, counting surely on this forcing him to flight. At the splash so near him, he drew back, seeming to rise on his feet on the water, lifted his wings, then instantly folded them, plunging forward and diving again; but in the flash I was quite sure that something was wrong with one of his wings. The next morning, I noticed among the local items of a daily paper published in the first town of any size on the river that a hunter had shot a loon which he found on the river unable to fly because of a damaged wing. Then I thought that the bird had been slightly wounded, while on wing with his flock, and had taken to the river as his only means of travelling when he could not fly.

In my present location, in the summer of 1917, a pair of loons nested on the lake shore about half a mile above the Cabin, making the only nest I have had personal experience with in Indiana.

In the winter of 1902, a farmer living near the Limberlost region brought to the Cabin the body of a large white Arctic owl which he had shot while it was perching on one of his fences. We sent the bird, its feathers a moving mass of tiny, red lice, to a taxidermist, and it came back beautifully mounted. No doubt it is still in this man's possession. That same winter the papers described the finding of a number of these birds in Ohio and Indiana, where they were most uncommon.

A sister, who was with me at the time I definitely decided to make my permanent home on the lake where I live to-day, declares that I paid the purchase price for an acre of blue-eyed grass, which I acquired with my holdings. She is only partly right. A wood duck also figured in the equation. Two different times I saw him riding the water dressed like the favorite of the Shah of Persia. He floated among the lily pads of a small bay on the bank of which his mate nested, only a few rods from my purchase. So I bought the wood duck and the blue-eyed grass, with a wealth of tall hardwood trees for good measure.

Linnaeus called this duck "the bride," but he should have explained that the male wore the nuptial dress and that the dress was that of the most colorful orientals; for this loveliest of our ducks is as gorgeous in dress as "Solomon in all his glory." My bird's beak, with its very dark, hooked, pointed tip, had a triangle of blood-red on each side at the base; from that a wide irregular mark of pale yellow ran down the sides. The top of his head was exquisite. It was pure green of several shades in places, bronze-maroon in others, bronzy green between. White lines ran from the red at the base of the beak above the eye on each side to the tip of the long crest, which hung far down the back of the neck. Secondary lines of white started back of the eyes and ended with the crest. The eyes were large, having wide circles of red around the iris. The cheeks and sides of the head were dark bronze. The throat was snow white, this color rounding the cheek and running up to the eye in a narrow strip, again circling the side of the head and coming to a point at the crest. The white came far down the throat, and stopped at an even line where the breast changed to a lovely shade of maroon, lighter than that of the head, yet having the same bronzy tints. This broad band covered the back of the neck below the shoulders, shading lighter over the crop, where it was flecked with almost invisible feathers of white at the top, the line widening and the feathers growing larger where they met the white underparts. At the wing butts, a narrow band of white faced the maroon, then one twice as wide of black; then came delicate pale yellow feathers finely traced with black, and broader bands of black and white. The back was green overlaid with maroon and hints of yellow, with a white band across the top of the tail base, the tail very long for a duck, green above, maroon at the sides. The feet were invisible in the water.

I used every caution to observe the bird closely without flushing it, as it was the only one I ever had seen in freedom, although my father knew this duck well when it was plentiful. He said it flew among the trees around water as gracefully as any bird, and walked large limbs lengthwise. This comes from its habit of nesting in cavities in large trees near or over the water. Our ornithology knows no lovelier bird, yet it is now close extinction through the greed of hunters and farmers. If it is not especially and rigorously protected, soon it will be lost to the world forever; and it is the handsomest duck alive, not excepting its near relative the Chinese mandarin.

Two days after my purchase was concluded, the duck was shot by a fisherman having a gun concealed in his boat – shot during the heart of the nesting season of June. In this same way vanished the last lovely wood pigeon, and the wild turkeys are going fast. If the men do not take active conservation measures soon, I shall be forced to enter politics to plead for the conservation of the forests, wildflowers, the birds, and over and above everything else, the precious water on which our comfort, fertility, and life itself depend.

CHAPTER VII - UNUSUAL EXPERIENCES AFIELD

ABOUT the time of the publication of "The Song of the Cardinal" a man in Indianapolis published a sharp criticism of my natural history, because I had described these birds as occasionally eating a stray bug or worm. He said that the cardinal grosbeak was named for its heavy sharp beak, which is especially designed for crushing seeds, so everyone knew that these birds were seed-eaters. So they are, as a rule, but all cardinals with which I have been intimately acquainted during a lifetime of experience have taken a few bugs and worms to change their diet, while in captivity they greet a bit of fresh scraped beefsteak with every sign of intense pleasure. The one lure that I found most effective in attracting cardinals to given locations before set cameras was to wire bits of bright red fresh beefsteak to the shrubbery I had in focus. Every woman who has ever kept a canary as a pet knows that this bird will sicken and die if she does not intersperse its staple diet of seed with lettuce leaves and apple; and unless canaries are given scraped beefsteak in the spring at the brooding time they will pull out their feathers and nibble the ends of them, so ravenous are they for the taste of meat.

This criticism set me to watching the seed-eaters afield particularly, and I soon learned that there was not one of them that did not vary its diet with fruit or a few berries and a bug or a worm here and there. On one occasion I saw one black vulture from a nest of which I was making a series of pictures in the Limberlost, fly down into a fence corner and eat a quantity of catnip leaves. A few days later I saw its mate snipping grass. Every one has seen dogs eat grass, and every cat lover knows what a treat catnip is to a cat. Both vultures ate freely of a handful of red raspberries I once placed in the mouth of their log; while every summer the kingfishers that fish around my stretch of lake shore in front of the Cabin, north, come into the wild cherry trees and eat fruit.

I once dug open the nest of a kingfisher in an embankment, after the young had left it, in order to measure the circumference of the nest room and the length of the tunnel, and to examine carefully the structure of the nest. It seemed to be formed entirely of regurgitated pellets that the brooding bird had ejected in a circle around her during incubation. Microscopic examination proved that nine tenths of the nest wall were the bones and scales of small fish; the other tenth was about equally divided between berry seeds and the bony structure of grasshoppers.

I one day picked up the body of a dead kingfisher in a section near the Limberlost, which I called Paradise Alley. Hunters were not allowed there, and the region was devoted solely to my work by its owner, who did all in his power to keep even fishermen and boys playing during their summer vacation out of the long wooded stretch where I had the greatest number of nests located; so I could not imagine what had happened to the bird. I could find no broken bones, no marks on its body, no displacement of plumage. It seemed to have starved to death, as its body was emaciated, so I took time to dissect it. I found that the trouble had been caused in regurgitating the bones of an unusually large fish. These birds swallow whole fish, tossing them in air and catching them headfirst so that they go down smoothly. The coming up seemed to have been another matter, with this bird at least, for a large sharp bone from a back fin had turned crosswise in the food canal near where it enters the crop, and was firmly imbedded in the flesh in such a way that the bird could not regurgitate the indigestible parts nor take other food.

Owls swallow their food in the same way, taking whatever prey they can whole, assimilating the digestible parts and regurgitating bones, fur, and feathers. Of course in the case of an owl, a hawk, or an eagle carrying away prey too large to swallow whole, that food is torn up and eaten in pieces. One of the most disagreeable experiences I ever had afield was in moving a dead calf which I found in our woods, about two miles farther south to the location of the black vulture. I hoped by placing that delectable vulture feast near the nest to coax the birds to become so tame that I could picture them feeding on the carcass; but the man who was a tenant on the land spoiled my scheme by burying the calf and ordering me not to make his land a dumping place for the stock that died on mine. I went so far as to tell him that I put the calf there for bird-food, but I was afraid to point out the vulture location or explain exactly what I was doing, because there was every probability that he would immediately take his gun and shoot the birds. He was a man who charged me a fee for driving down a lane and following a road through the swamp, which he and the oilmen of the region used every day. I should like to add that he is the only man in all of my years of field work who ever did this.

On the disagreeable subject of unusual food taken by birds: in company with my brother-in-law, driving from one village to another in southern Michigan I one day watched a red-shouldered hawk killing a snake. He was using the methods attributed to the eagle, which dropped from aloft the tortoise that struck the head and caused the death of the poet Aeschylus. This very unkind proceeding is described as having taken place in an open field where the poet had sought refuge upon a day when it had been predicted that he would meet his death by something falling upon his head. In an open field I saw the hawk rising from the ground, in its talons the body of a long blacksnake squirming and twisting. The bird ascended in almost perpendicular flight to a height perhaps three times that of the tallest trees bordering the field. It dropped the snake and plunged headlong after

51

it, reaching the ground at practically the same time. It immediately caught up the stunned snake, mounting again even higher than before, where it again dropped its prey. When the hawk took up the snake the next time its body hung straight and limp, so the bird sailed away toward an adjoining piece of tall timber.

Another time I saw only a part of the efforts of a hawk to secure a dinner which made a very amusing spectacle. I was riding north on the Grand Rapids and Indiana Railway, when I saw a big chicken hawk drop on a chicken, which was about three fourths grown – or if full-grown, a small hen. The hen saw the hawk in time to make a frantic plunge for the shelter of a snake fence, separating two fields. She came so near being caught that the interested passengers on the train could see her feathers fall from the hawk's talons as he arose. The chicken gained the fence and darted through a crack. The hawk arose and dropped on the other side of the fence. The chicken turned and again struggled between the rails, before the hawk reached it. When the train carried us from sight this performance was still going on. I walked to the back of the ear to watch the struggle as long as possible; when I could no longer distinguish what was happening, the chicken had crept through the fence crack for the fifth time. I am unable to say whether it eventually escaped or not, but I have an idea that the hawk finally succeeded in catching the chicken, which was in a panic.

Another peculiar and intensely interesting instance of feeding in the wild occurred in a bit of swamp which lies almost directly across the lake from Limberlost Cabin, north. Every season red-winged blackbirds nest among the water willows, marsh grasses, and cat-tails of this swamp, but one season, four years ago, a large flock took possession of this stretch of swamp, remaining there until they left with their young after they were able to fly for a combined attack on the grain fields of the region. While slowly pushing a boat around the outside of this swamp, searching for a red-wing nest, I saw one of these birds alight on a branch of water willow and lean down to the water either to pick up something on the surface or to take a drink. He chose his location without exercising any judgment or using the precaution of examining the water carefully. More quickly than I could tell the story, a big black bass sprang one third of its length out of the water, snapped its huge jaws shut on the blackbird, and disappeared. This is the only time I ever saw a fish take a bird for food, but the following season I dressed a four and one half pound black bass the stomach of which contained a red-wing blackbird. The stomach of another large bass I once dressed contained a sunfish fully as large as my hand.

My daughter and I one day, attracted by a commotion among the flowers at the end of the steps, saw a red squirrel run for the distance of a rod over the earth and then climb a wild cherry tree, carrying in its mouth the squirming, struggling body of a field mouse. A few weeks later, a red squirrel from the nest in this same tree caught a ground squirrel across the back and despite the little fellow's cries and struggles he was carried up the tree and forced headfirst into the opening, which goes to prove that squirrels vary their customary diet of nuts with some meat. I have also seen them eat berries and fruit. If my strawberry bed could speak, it could "a tale relate" as to the depredations of squirrels, mice, ground hogs, birds, ants, bees, and bugs. The bed has to be unusually large so that any berries are left for us.

Writing of fish recalls the fact that, while working in the Valley of the Wood Robin beside the Wabash, a few days after the water of a high flood had subsided one spring, I found the body of a large carp firmly impaled on a thorn tree. The fish evidently had been carried sidewise by the stiff swirl of the current, as the thorn was driven squarely into its side and penetrated the entire body.

One of the most peculiar nests it has fallen to my lot to work around was originally built by a shitepoke. It rested in the sharply branching crotch of a young elm tree, where two small limbs had grown out from the side of the trunk, and from the pressure of the surrounding thicket had kept nearly parallel with the trunk of the tree. The entire structure started in this narrow crotch, widening as the limbs spread until it was fully twenty inches in height. Toward the top the sticks used in the outer wall were the thickness of a lead pencil and two feet in length – a few of them even longer. The nest was so weather-beaten that it undoubtedly had stood for several seasons, and it was so firmly constructed that it gave promise of standing for as many more. Using this structure as a foundation, a yellow-billed cuckoo had begun in the nesting cavity and built her usual nest, a few sticks and twigs loosely laid, with a slight lining of dried willow catkins and the down of last year's weed growth. At the time I first investigated the nest it contained four beautiful big cuckoo eggs. The nest made such a lovely picture I hastily set up my highest step-ladder, and from the top of it, about level with the top of the nest, I reproduced the structure from the lowest to the highest twig used in building it.

There have been a few times in field work, while I was on the editorial staff of Outing doing some magazine work or particularly pressed for some special picture needed to complete the work of illustrating an article or book, when I have had such rare luck in securing a subject that I almost felt encouraged to believe that the Lord was with me, and putting it into the hearts of the wild creatures to come at my call and give me exactly the pose wanted. Very distinctly in my memory there stands out one day when I especially desired the picture of an owl. I was not particular what kind or what size, for a screech owl can look quite as dignified and wise as its great horned cousin of the big woods. I had been writing an article on what the birds know, and I wanted an owl head for a first paragraph inset as this bird is always used when a bird picture is wanted to illustrate wisdom – not that the owl is by any means the wisest bird of the woods for it happens to be one of the most stupid, but like a great many people, if it will consent to keep its mouth shut and content itself with merely looking wise it serves the purpose admirably.

The time was in early December. All day I cudgeled my brain to think where or how I could secure a study of an owl to complete my article. About nine o'clock that night, passing through the back row of rooms in the Cabin, south, next to the orchard, I heard a screech owl calling very close. Not long before, I had come as nearly perfecting myself as was possible in owl notes for a recitation I intended to give. I turned out the lights, darkening the entire back part of the house; lowered the upper sash of a kitchen window; lighted a candle to make a dim glow, screening it with a piece of pasteboard – so that it would have the effect of diffused light from the outside; and then crouched beneath the window. After listening carefully, I began low imitations of the bird's cries with all the exactitude possible to me. After a few efforts I felt sure that the bird was answering me, so I waited, as nearly as I could gauge, the same interval of time he did, and kept up the calls, carefully intoning and accenting, encouraged by the fact that the calls outside were beyond question drawing nearer. I think that my heart stood quite still for a second, when there was a shadow above my head. Instantly, I arose, pushed shut the window, and turned to find the owl sitting on the back of one of the kitchen chairs, steadily gazing at the light. He had the freedom of the kitchen until morning, as I dared not put him in the conservatory with the canary house. The following day, when he was bewildered by the light and unusual location, I reproduced him, back, front, and sides, in every posture I could imagine an owl might assume in freedom; and as soon as it was dusk I opened the door and I gave him freedom. Then I developed my plates, and the following day my completed article was on its way to the publisher. Several times after that I amused visitors at the Cabin by calling screech owls in at the open window merely to prove that it was possible.

Frequently in field work I have met with cases of birds and animals trusting to protective coloration for security. There have been times when I think I could have picked up a rabbit while he was playing this game, had there been any object in so doing. Beyond all question the most complete instance of the kind happened on the lake on which we live. One spring morning my husband came in saying that the black bass were "bait-fighting" by which he meant that while the females were preparing their nests and getting ready to spawn, the males were in shallow water making mad rushes at anything that struck the surface. I knew that he wanted me to row the boat for him while he would cast, at least one trip, around the head of the lake. Without stopping to think of anything except fishing I took my rod and stepped into the boat. After rowing around our lake I rounded the point of a big island lying in front of us, crossed the branch of the lake on the far side of it, and started around that shore line. At this point my husband took the oars and I began to cast. We had proceeded up the lake shore through the narrows and dropped back around the side of a bay near an old water tank, used by the Grand Rapids and Indiana Railway Company when they had a dummy track laid at the head of the lake to bring out gravel for the construction of the road. Not far below the tank, in a sort of pocket formed by a big log extending from the shore into the water and bordered by cat-tails, bulrushes, and several kinds of swamp grasses, in glancing ahead I saw a beautiful big brown bittern quite close to us. He was wading along the lake shore, lifting his feet silently, setting them down carefully, his beak not far from the surface, intent on watching the water for small fish, frogs or worms for his breakfast as he advanced. At the same instant I saw him he saw the boat.

I cautioned my husband not to move a muscle not absolutely necessary, to propel the boat as I directed, and to use great care to lift the oars slowly and lower them quietly. That was the first time in years that I had started to do anything afield or on the water without a snapshot camera in my hand. Before me was an opportunity to take a splendid picture of one of our most attractive water birds, which would have the added value of giving its exact pose when trusting to protective coloration, exactly what this bird was doing; for the instant he saw me he stopped as if petrified in his tracks, compressed his feathers to his body so tightly that he appeared not more than half of his original size, drew down his neck and pointed his beak almost straight up, putting his entire body into a position as nearly perpendicular as possible. He was only a few inches from his grassy background, while the morning sun was shining directly on him, for he was on the north bank of the lake. I said to my husband: "I have no camera, but let me make a test of what I could do if I had one." Slowly dropping to my knees I picked up a tackle box in the bottom of the boat, pulled to me a coat which my husband had discarded, set the tackle box on the seat where I had been sitting, and, using the coat for a dark-cloth, I went through every motion that would have been required to set up a camera, focus it, expose, and change plates. The bird stood motionless. I suggested to my husband that he carefully move the boat five or six feet closer, then again I went through the performance of taking a picture. We repeated this several times, until my end of the boat was exactly ten feet from the bird. I could not see that an eyelid quivered or that he moved the tip of a feather; nor did I see any reason for flushing him, because there was a faint hope that I might come around the lake shore some other morning and find him in the same spot, when I was prepared to reproduce his likeness. So with exactly the same caution we had used in approaching him we slipped away and left him there. As far as I could distinguish the bird from his background he remained motionless.

It would be impossible to make anyone who had not seen this bird in the same location believe how completely he became a part of his surroundings when he threw himself into position. His bare, slender feet and legs were greenish yellow exactly like the grass-shaded water and the sands on which he stood. His breast was striped in even bands, almost exactly the width of the blades of marsh grass, seeming as if it had been measured and penciled – one stripe precisely the yellowish tan of last year's dead leaf, the next stripe the richer brown of an older leaf having had longer exposure to the weather. His eyes were rimmed with pale yellow, with yellow rings around the iris, while his upturned beak was almost too good to be true. On his throat was the tan of the grasses, on his head exactly their brown, while the large, sharply pointed beak itself was striped with this tan shading to brighter yellow, with the green of the bulrushes, the paler tannish green of the cattails faintly lined with a touch of dull red exactly reproducing the rust-red effect of some of the grasses, and the extreme tip of the beak was the same old ivory as the dead outer leaves from which this year's fresh cat-tails were springing. For the remainder of that season I frequently hunted him along this same stretch of lake shore, and while I often saw him flying over the lake or alighting in bays opposite me, I never again succeeded in getting within working distance of him at a time when I was prepared for work.

A pitiful and peculiar bird experience occurred in my presence on a lake in Michigan where I was rowing a boat while my brother-in-law, with an artificial minnow, was making a series of particularly long and expert casts for bass. As straight as if it had been shot from a gun a swallow darted in front of the flying bait, which struck it squarely and there was nothing to do but to reel in and attempt its release. From the impact of the bait at nearly a hundred feet, being dragged through the water for the length of the cast, and the pain of having most of the hooks deeply imbedded in its body, the bird was dead before it reached the boat I hope. It was so terribly abused and wounded that I made sure that it was beyond suffering before attempting to remove the hooks. A man might try for an average lifetime to strike a bird on wing at that distance with an artificial bait and not succeed in hitting it. It is scarcely necessary to say that neither of us would have had this accident occur for any consideration if we could have prevented it, as swallows are particularly inoffensive and peculiarly graceful and attractive birds in flight, while their benefit in winnowing the air of countless gnats, mosquitoes, and almost invisible winged pests is beyond calculation.

CHAPTER VIII - UNUSUAL EXPERIENCES AFIELD

IN COMPANY with half a dozen other women, I was driving home from a near-by village where we had spent the night with a friend. We stopped and watched, until we had no more time to spend, a sight as unusual as I ever have seen in the woods. In a dense piece of woods well toward the foot of the Limberlost country, on a heavy limb topping a stack of wind-fall brush there perched the biggest and oldest great horned owl of my experience. Because I was so particularly interested in birds, my friends waited while I climbed the snake fence and cautiously crept through the woods until, screened by the thicket only a few yards away, I could distinctly see what was going on. Again, I had no camera with me, and there was too much shade for the constant motion of the subject besides. The owl was in some physical trouble just what, I could not discover, but he had every appearance of being almost ready to die of old age. In a long, well-fed life, he had grown to magnificent proportions, which probably appeared double, because every feather on him was standing on end. These feathers were grey with age. He showed scarcely a trace of the dark or even the lighter brown shades of his species, being more of a dirty white and washed-out greyish tan. His big feet and huge nails, and his toes and legs seemed to be encrusted with scale, probably contracted by lack of cleanliness after having torn up prey with them; for he was big enough and had the strength to handle a chicken, a small pig, or even a newborn lamb, although I never heard of an owl taking such animals. His eyes were wide open as was his mouth. He constantly uttered a hissing sound, rapidly turning his head from side to side as he snapped at a bevy of small birds that were tormenting him. Forgetting everything else – even their fear of each other – all of the denizens of that woods had collected around the owl. Prominent among his tormentors were two crows, two or three blue jays, several kingbirds, while further removed, yet not failing to take a peck at him occasionally, were a number of robins. Several orioles were surprisingly pugnacious. There were a number of sparrows and even little things like warblers and vireos. One summer yellow bird made a streak of light as he dashed chattering past the owl's head, and several wrens were jabbering insanely when they darted in among the other birds. Perhaps the most amazing feature of the spectacle to me was that in combining against the owl all of these smaller birds were fighting in perfect accord with the crows, and in the half hour or possibly longer that I detained my party to watch this performance I never once saw the crows make the slightest aggressive move against any of the other birds.

It would be a wonderful thing if I could make you see the great horned owl in a frenzy of anger and fear, hissing and snapping right and left, his head seeming positively to turn a complete circle on his neck when the most impudent of the tormentors actually flew against his head and shoulders and succeeded in pulling a feather from him in passing. He made repeated strokes at them, hissing and threatening constantly, even striking with the butts of his half-lifted wings a motion I never before saw an owl make in self-defense, while circling around him, darting over and at him, each uttering the high, shrill alarm call of his kind, flashed the black bodies of the crows and blackbirds, the blue of jays, the brown and grey of the sparrows, the steel of the kingbirds and wood pewees, and the gold of the orioles and summer yellow birds. At the time I left, so slow were the movements of the owl and so imperfect seemed his sight that he had not succeeded in pulling even a feather from one of his tormentors. I never have been able to rid myself of the feeling that the owl's time as a fighter was almost over, on account of the condition of his beak and feet and his plumage. Of course I made allowance for the fact that the strong coloring on a bird is usually confined to a very small touch on the extreme tip of the feathering, the deep effect resulting from these thickly overlapping. Any bird with its feathers standing on end so that the greater part of the feather and the downy covering next the flesh show naturally appears much lighter and of different color than when the feathers are folded; but even making all due allowance in this respect, I still maintain that the owl of this encounter was a patriarch very near the close of his days.

Writing of this owl reminds me of three other instances in which I have seen birds of many species mass to attack a common enemy. One of my neighbour boys had a crow that he had taken from a nest and was raising by hand. This bird had the freedom of the neighborhood and even came to visit me at the Cabin, where I frequently gave him food if I had anything convenient for which I thought he would care. One morning while passing through the kitchen I heard a small pandemonium going on in the back yard. On investigating, I found the crow perched on a lower crosspiece of the grape arbor, while taking a peck at him in flight as they passed, were the orioles from a nest in a pear tree across the alley, my bluebirds from a box on the abour, a pair of wrens that had a house on the arbor, the martins from the windmill, and the robins from half a dozen nests, while there was a liberal sprinkling of English sparrows, which were always hanging around ready for any mischief they might do. The crow solved his difficulties by spreading his wings and flying home.

Once in a big field beside the Wabash River, my field assistant, my daughter, and I watched a pair of kingbirds and several other birds, smaller but flying so high we could not differentiate them without field glasses, fly after and over a big hawk, the kingbirds constantly dropping to pick its head and eyes, then rising straight in the air. At times, they seemed actually to perch on its back between its shoulders, but the height was so great and the flight of the hawk so rapid I could not state positively that they did this.

The first summer that we lived in our present Cabin, an immense flock of red-winged blackbirds nested in the reeds in a small bay directly across the lake from us. A pair of big grey and tan chicken hawks had their nest somewhere in the tall timber of Kestler's Island high above the bay. Throughout the summer these hawks hung above the cattails and bulrushes, swooping down as often as they were hungry, almost never failing to carry prey as they arose to sail back to the woods. Then with angry cries, practically the whole male population of the swamp would arise and pursue the hawks. Sometimes crows would come to the assistance of the red-wings, but so long as they remained about their nesting affairs so long the hawks preyed upon them. When the red-wings were gone, the hawks merely dropped lower and made their attacks on the grebe, the cinereous coot, and the other water birds swimming around the edges of the marsh with their young.

One of the most exquisite birds I ever had in my fingers was carried to me a few seasons ago by my driver. It had flown in the open door of the garage, and was beating itself on an opposite window, unable to find its way out. It had battered itself until it was so tired that he was able to pick it up and carry it to me. It was a chestnut-sided warbler, having a white throat, yellow cap, white beak, chestnut sides, and half a dozen different shades running from white to steel grey over its wings. In a few minutes it revived so that it was able to fly.

Mentioning this driver recalls the fact that he told me on several occasions that there was a stray cat which had been abandoned by some of the cottagers at the head of the lake and left to run the woods until it had returned to the wild, or there was some kind of prowling animal of the cat species in the woods behind the garage, where he said at times its screams almost "raised the hair of his head." One night the screams came particularly early, so he hurried down to the veranda to call me. I went with him to the woods, very shortly located his screamer, and was able to satisfy him that it was merely one of our great horned owls uttering one of its most blood-curdling cries, when it flew with wings widely spread into a clump of bushes to drive out some of the cardinals, warblers, or other small birds that might be nesting or perching there. I have no doubt that other stories carried to me of some wild animal's infesting our northern Indiana woods and making the night hideous with its screams had their origin in nothing more than a hungry horned owl's using this original method to scare up prey.

While orchid hunting one day on the banks of one of the most beautiful lakes in northern Indiana – or in the world for that matter – on a moss-covered log far back among the dim tamaracks deep in the ooze and slime

59

of the swamp, I caught a glimpse of an exquisite shade of rose-color. Almost at the same time, our State Entomologist, who was engaged in field work with me, saw it also. Each of us started by a different route to make our way toward it, climbing over rotten logs, clinging to button bushes or swamp holly, or recklessly supporting ourselves with poison sumac. We at last reached the log at practically the same time to see embedded among the exquisite fine moss and lichens covering it, a thickly pedaled flower shaped much like a wild rose, lying flat and completely surrounded by the mosses, among which it bloomed. Stooping to try to trace its root system in order to identify it, I discovered that it was a pink rose, blown of glass, very probably carried to its location far in the swamp by a crow, where it had lain until the moss crept up and so surrounded it that even standing above it anyone would have mistaken it for a natural flower. I brought our wonderful rose home where I keep it among my mementoes of field work, because I especially enjoy a good joke on myself.

Last season my husband came to me and said he wanted my interpretation of a piece of natural history that was worrying him. Between the parks in which he kept his crested Polish and white Plymouth Rock chickens, he had found the gate-pin hole completely corked with tiny bits of wood. I went with him and watched him take his penknife and remove the little pieces. Behind them we found the hole packed full of beechnuts, so I told him to watch for a few days and see what bird he found there. Before the day was over he came to tell me that a downy woodpecker was busy refilling the hole with more bits of wood, which it was collecting for the purpose.

I might add among peculiar experiences afield the history of a picture I made in a lake only a short distance from Silver Lake, Indiana. The shores of this lake, I was told by natives, were badly infested with a snake I have not yet been able to identify, which they called "red-bellies," and persistently asserted their bite meant instant death; so I was constantly warned by my guide to watch out for snakes and to be very careful. With my paraphernalia in a boat, the guide rowing around the lake shore, wherever I found a subject on which I wanted to work and could not manage efficiently from the boat, I climbed out in the water, after testing its depth with an oar, and set up my camera in the muck. This was particularly messy business, fraught with dangers of going under in a fretwork of muskrat burrows or quicksand, but I was collecting illustrations for a portion of a book devoted to swamp subjects and the only place to secure my illustration was swampy lake shore or inland swamp; so there was nothing to do but forget the discomforts and absorb myself beyond any other thought in the work of securing my pictures. When I had set up my camera, and focused it on the subject, it was my custom to take an exposure bulb with several yards of hose attached in my hand or let it float on the water, while I went forward and put the bed of flowers or whatever composed my picture into the best shape possible by removing out-of-focus limbs, flowers, or leaves from the foreground, straightening out the whole subject into the most artistic composition possible to me. One particular stretch of lake shore was thickly covered with pickere weed at the height of bloom, with its background of higher bushes and arrow-head lilies, while a rippling current in the water before it made a particularly exquisite picture. I walked the length of this bed, bending over it, pulling out some growth I did not want, here and there removing leaves that were too prominent. It seemed in retrospection that there was not a foot of the bed in which I did not have my fingers. Ten days afterward, at home in my dark-room developing these plates, I was amazed to see in the midst of this picture, lifting its head and with open mouth, a snake, his fangs plainly showing; so I must have made the exposure at the very instant at which he struck at me and hit a lily leaf instead. - I had been intent on my footing or the camera so that I did not see him; and I should have paid no attention to slight motion in a composition of this kind, because I was constantly running on to musk-rats, ground-puppies, frogs, and water snakes while working in such locations.

On the subject of snakes, I must add one other incident of my career. The little boy, Billy, described in "A Girl of the Limberlost" was a very real character, the truth being that the incidents attributed to him in the home of the Sintons really occurred at the Cabin, south. He was a brave little soul, faithful beyond telling, entirely devoted to me and to my daughter. One morning during a midsummer of intense heat he heard me express a desire for rain. He immediately remarked: "I can get the rain for you," to which I questioned: "How can you get it, Billy?"

He answered: "Mrs. Smith says that if you kill a snake and turn its belly up, it will rain before night. I know where I can always find a snake, 'cause us boys go snake-hunting lots of times. I can get you rain."

I answered: "Oh, no, you can't, Billy. That is a silly, old superstition."

Shortly afterward, Billy disappeared without telling me where he was going. About half past three in the afternoon, he returned, an object demanding an immediate tubbing. His face was red, his neck and hands brier-scratched. He was dirty beyond belief, but his small features shone with a look of confident triumph.

"Now you'll get your rain," he said conclusively. "I found a good big snake, and I have killed it and laid it right out in the road, where everybody can see it!"

The sky was cloudless, the sun shining clear. I said to him: "What nonsense! Killing a snake never made rain!"

"It didn't?" shouted Billy. "Oh, but look out the window!"

I turned to the window and to my utter confusion saw the rain pelting down in big drops that splattered on the walks as it fell straight from a clear sky.

I do not recall the exact date, but it was a season from eight to ten years ago during which we experienced the most peculiar rainfall I ever have seen. Half a dozen times during that summer rain f-ll from a clear sky enough to wet the sidewalks and grass at the Cabin, while the main street of the village, two blocks away, was dry. These rains were often so local that at one time my sidewalk on our side of the street was quite wet, while my neighbor's across the street had not a drop.

My husband and I, sitting on the veranda one Sabbath afternoon shortly after dinner, saw one of these local rains falling a short distance east of us, over an area that looked to be no larger than an average building lot in a village. At the same time the martins on our windmill behind the house saw it, and high in a flock they began taking a bath in air by flying through the rainfall, turning and plunging into it again. They kept this up with constant chatter and manifest delight until they attracted the attention of a large flock of chimney swallows, living in the belfry of the village school-house about two blocks away, air line. The swallows came chattering, dozens of them in a flock, and dashed into the rain for a bath or a drink on wing. All of this time, the sun was shining brightly almost directly behind our backs so that the falling drops were tinted in rainbow lights, and the bodies of the birds, heading into the water, seemed to be bordered with rainbow colors, making one of the most exquisite sights imaginable.

Crossing a field in the region of the Limberlost late one afternoon in fall, in approaching a road I heard a confusion of bird voices, all seeming to belong to the warbler family. Keeping behind some bushes on my side of the fence, I crept up and so drew very close to a wonderful picture. In a line on a wire fence, there was a string the length of a city lot, of warblers gathering for migration, while over several bushes before and close behind the fence flocked dozens upon dozens more of these trim exquisite little birds. Of course, the predominant color was yellow, there being the pure gold of the summer yellow bird and the slightly deeper shade of the prothonotary. There were the deep orange of the Blackburnian and the mottled yellow of the magnolian. There appeared prominently on the wire the yellow head and throat of the blue-wing, the stronger touch of yellow of the redstart, the black-throated green warbler, the yellow pine and the yellow-touched hood and mourning warblers. There were a number of specimens of the black-throated blue warbler and the still paler cerulean. There was at least one specimen of the bay-breasted warbler, with robin-breast color on the top of its head and all over its underparts, and there were enough chattering, little warblers I could not identify to have made a large flock. I do not profess to be acquainted with all of the warblers of my locality. When one takes into consideration that in almost no instance are the male and female alike, while a flock collecting for migration might contain more than half of its members in the form of young birds, which until a first moulting would not resemble either of the parents, it can readily be understood how bewildered I, or any other field worker, would have been. The birds seemed to wait on the wire and bushes for several minutes, while numbers of their kind joined them from small bushes over the field and the adjoining woods. The whole flock seemed excited, on high nervous tension, and constantly chirped and chattered. In a short time, as one bird they took wing, rising higher than I ever had seen warblers fly about the business of living, and headed due south. As a rare and unusual sight I can think of no experience in field work to surpass the beauty of this picture.

In the spring of 1918 at the Cabin, north, on a warm May Sabbath morning, with occasional showers falling, the cook came to ask me to go to the back porch. All of the warblers described in the previous instance had returned to the North in a body, and having just landed in the dense tangles of vines climbing over the high growth above the spring, they paused to hold a Sabbath service of thanksgiving for their safe arrival. For several hours – until midafternoon, in fact – a rolling, trilling volume of sound ascended from the region of the spring. Then it ceased, and after that not more than a dozen could be heard at one time.

Two other instances of particularly exquisite things I have seen in nature occurred on my own premises at Limberlost Cabin, south. One was the mating of a pair of Baltimore orioles. They had selected a nest location in a cottonwood across the street, but they were bathing, feeding, and gathering nest material on our premises. I was standing in the conservatory talking with my daughter and a New York friend who was visiting me, when the female oriole flew to a beautiful specimen of Killarney rose bush growing against the west fence, which we had changed from the original broad boards to a high wall, laid up with large blocks of Wabash River limestone. Behind the green foliage of the rose bearing blooms of magnificent size, one being seven inches in diameter, the cream stone of the wall made a perfect background for the cutting of the rose leaves and the luscious pink blooms, while in front of it spread a fine sweep of turfy lawn grass. Like a meteor of gold the female bird dropped from high flight to the rose bush. Almost a-wing with her flashed the orange and black of the male. He perched beside her and they locked beaks in a long caress. I had not known before that orioles locked bills in their love making and I do not know now that they do in every instance. Three of us distinctly saw what occurred in the incident I am describing. The female fluttered to the delicate green grass, her wings half-lifted and outspread, her head turned to one side, her beak lifted. The male followed her in a frenzy of the mating fever, repeatedly kissing her, delicately stroking her wing feathers, finally consummating his mating.

The other case when I was present at the finale of the love affairs of a pair of birds occurred with a pair of cardinal grosbeaks that were building a nest in a wild rose bush climbing over the music-room windows. The foundations of the nest were laid and one day had been spent by the female in industrious work. Toward evening she left the location, flying east, probably on her way to the river to hunt for food or to get a drink. During her absence the male bird flew to a lower branch of a big elm tree in a corner of the dooryard, not far from where I was sitting in company with a friend on the front steps. The western light struck him fully, lighting his plumage to its most gorgeous coloring, touching his black beard with lights of silver. He called and chirped inquiringly. Getting no answer from the rose bush he flew there to investigate. Not finding his mate there he returned to the perch on the elm tree. Almost as he reached it the female came flying from the east, and, in answer to his calls, joined him on the elm branch. Immediately, he burst into his most impassioned strain of song. He lifted his head, swelling his throat, flaring his crest to the utmost, half lifting his wings, rocking from side to side, turning and twisting on the limb before her, displaying his coloring and his grace to the utmost advantage, while note for note he threw all the tenderness and pleading and passion of his heart into his vocal performance. He stressed each note to its highest reach, its most poignant pleading, its mellowest tone, with impassioned gestures, singing and whistling his complete repertoire; when the hen bird gave a faint cheep of assent, as his notes died to a mere whisper of sound in his throat, their mating was accomplished.

During a fall expedition in nest collecting made as a basis for the chapter of this book entitled "Nest Building," with my clippers I once cut the main twig of a small thicket of oak sprouts growing around the stump of a tree long felled, to collect what I imagined was a leaf-filled catbird nest. As the severed nest tipped toward me, I caught it with one hand and received directly in my face and over my breast the father, mother, and half a dozen young from a nest of field mice. After recovering from a shock which any woman will understand and few men would covet, I examined the nest to find that it was securely roofed with large sycamore leaves woven and firmly fastened to the outer edge of the nest. The nest cavity under this roof was filled with grasses, feathers, fur, and down. At one side there was a round hole about the size of a silver quarter, which was at a spot convenient for the mice to enter by running up the stem and following out one branch that passed beside the opening.

CHAPTER IX – RARE PICTURES AFIELD

AMONG the rarest pictures secured by an ornithological field worker I should not include those having wonderful backgrounds, good composition, atmosphere, or any fine example of pictorial art, but rather enumerate the reproduction directly from life of birds exhibiting some especial characteristic, performing some particularly intimate act of their lives, or in some pose which is of peculiar scientific value. In the illustration of my first book "The Song of the Cardinal," there are more instances of these things than in any other series of studies of the home life of a pair of birds that I have been fortunate enough to secure. In order to carry the pictorial history of these birds through the entire gamut of bird life I worked around every cardinal nest I could find for three years, using many lures to attract the birds before set cameras, such as wiring beefsteak to limbs and bushes, and subterfuges such as introducing lemon trees from my conservatory into the immediate surroundings of a nest so that I could secure reproductions of the birds portraying their time of residence in the South.

The very cream of these illustrations is two courting pictures, both of which were made near a nest on which I had worked for several weeks. At a time when the first of the young had flown, while the last remained a day longer in the nest, the old birds began courting, preliminary to building a new nest, the site which they had agreed upon being only a few rods down the river from the first nest in the same stretch of sumac thicket. These were genuine courting pictures, in each instance the birds having mated scarcely a second after the picture was taken. I also count as very rare the picture of this female at work on her second nest, as, for reasons I have explained, it is almost impossible to photograph the birds in the act of gathering material or weaving it into a nest they are building.

An unusual picture, and one I have had few other chances to secure, was the one of this series in which the male bird carried the female a morsel of food – I could not see what, but a seed or something hard – on which she bit for several seconds before she swallowed it. The picture was snapped while the hen was still nibbling the food. A few inches away, the male, after delivering the food, ran his beak down the length of her wing next him in what seemed to be a caress; then, with an expression of extreme solicitude on his face, watched her an instant before he took wing. I also made three pictures of this male cardinal standing guard on the edge of the nest while the female went to bathe and drink. Two of these were unusually interesting, one was an exposure showing his head turned to one side as a bird does when it is intently watching and listening; the other was taken immediately after a bath, while his wet feathers were so plastered to him in

65

patches that anyone not understanding the situation would marvel at his condition. This picture I did not include in the book, as I wished to use it for the frontispiece of another book exclusively on birds, for which I was gathering material at that time.

Another picture of extreme interest occurs twice in the book, where the male is photographed sidewise, his head turned directly toward the lens, his mouth open enough so that the curved line of his beak and the incisor, which might almost be the remnant of vanishing teeth, show. There is no way to estimate the scientific value of such a picture of a living bird, because the bird is shown in the freshness of life, and not in the dried, shrunken condition of a museum specimen. In each of these pictures the formation of the upper mandible also is clearly outlined. This series includes studies of the male bird with his feathers on end, his body tipped to such an angle as would allow the sun to shine on his skin, as birds place themselves for a sun bath. Another pose is without a suspicion of crest, his feathers plastered tight as they are held by the birds to keep a dash of rain from wetting the body. There are also several in the series of the male in full tide of song.

During the length of time I was at work collecting the illustrations for this book I made a photograph having all of the pictorial value possible to me, of every cardinal nest I could locate or that any of my friends could find for me. Many of these were of extreme beauty but none approached, from the points of beauty and historical value, that nest found by my daughter in the Valley of the Wood Robin, long after the complete illustration of the life history of these birds was assured, and at a time when the book was almost finished. We were working together, systematically searching through every shrub and bush for birds' nests, when her cry of delight brought me to her. She had flushed a hen cardinal, brooding in a thicket of wild rose growing over a stack of brush on an old stump at the edge of the swamp. It was not the swamp wild rose but the genuine sweetbrier with its pungent leaves, stout long climbing stems; and the immediate region of the nest was a mass of lovely pink blooms, shading from the deep red of the unfolded buds to the strong pink flowers just opened and the delicate pinkish white petals almost ready to fall. The hen bird of this nest could easily reach out and catch insects attracted by the sweetness of the bloom when she was brooding, while more could be had by rising to her feet or hopping to the edge of the nest.

I have made many series of pictures quite complete in historical value of the homes of most of our birds, but never a series to equal this one of the cardinals, which I carried to the farthest extent I possibly could on account of writing an entire book concerning one pair of birds. It will be easy for any naturalist, examining the pictures, to see that the birds are not the same pair throughout the illustration, although the story represents them to be.

A number of these pictures are not reproductions of our common Indiana redbird, but of the larger, brighter redbird of Kansas and Iowa, which for some reason had strayed into the Limberlost, found him a mate, and homed there for a season. He was an old bird of bloody red plumage, jetty beard, and having had so much association with man that he showed almost contempt for the cameras introduced into his vicinity. After a few days spent in becoming accustomed to me, he went about his affairs in utter disregard of my cameras, very frequently perching on them in leaving the nest, which he made a practice of entering from one direction, although he left it as the spirit moved him. This is a habit pertaining to all birds with which I ever have worked.

What is probably as good, if not the best, likeness of a bird I ever made afield, I got through this characteristic. I had my camera focused on the nest of a pair of kingbirds to which both of the old birds were coming constantly, each by a private route, to feed the young. The male at each approach to the nest flew to the end of a twig on which the nest was located. This branch was alive and small apples were sticking up around the nest, but the extreme tip, on which the bird alighted from a higher point in his route, was dead and bare so that every natural history point possible to include in one picture was shown almost every time he alighted. Noticing this, I decided to move the camera a few feet, focus it on the tip of the branch, and see if I could secure a picture of him during the instant he perched there before he flew to the nest. After he had left from one feeding I moved the camera, made the focus as sharp as possible, and retired to hiding. The picture I secured was made the first time he alighted on the twig. As he struck it, he noticed the camera was in a different position. He drew back his head, but did not move his body. The picture shows him breast toward the camera, his head slightly turned to one side, which resulted in giving the exact shape of his beak, his eye, the height and rounding of his crest, his wings not tightly folded to his sides, his feet both in view as they naturally grasped the twig, his tail widespread showing the white border, his pose alert. I scarcely see how it would be possible to crowd more interesting points into one reproduction of a bird, while on his face is plainly to be seen the curiosity he undoubtedly was experiencing as to what the camera was, and why the strange object had moved since his latest trip to the nest.

I regard a picture of a male bird brooding or standing guard on the edge of the nest as a real triumph; carrying food to his mate so that both old birds are included in the picture comes next; and third I would place a good picture of a male bird feeding his young, although it frequently happens that, with a camera focused on a nest, I have pictured both birds attending to the young at the same time.

Among my oriole pictures, I have made one that stands preeminent. In the first place the nest was very large, finely woven mostly of what I call natural material. Plant fiber and hair comprised the entire purse part of the nest with the exception of a long piece of cotton cord and one white carpet rag, which formed the anchorage at one side. The cord ran across the top of the nest, wound three or four times around a limb, then was tucked in and tied at the other end. It was carried perhaps an inch higher than the full length of the nest, where it was tightly lashed, fastened, and reinforced with plant fiber. The whole nest was very light in color, silver grey and white. When I made this exposure the young were old enough that their open beaks were lifted above the edge of the nest when they stood for feeding. The male bird flew into the tree. He alighted on the branch just above the lower edge of the nest, bringing his full breast and underparts, the underpart of his tail and under tip of his wings into view. The butt of one shoulder and full line of one wing appeared in the picture. His head was turned at such an angle that his upper and lower mandible were clearly cut; his eye shone like a bead of light; while his bill closed on a small, wiry worm, extending beyond it perhaps an inch on one side, and an inch and a half on the other. This picture I regard as very beautiful as well as rare.

Another of my favorites is a reproduction of a brooding cuckoo. Mr. Black had trained the bird with a soap box and coat by pretending to take her picture until she was so tame that after a few efforts with her, I was able to walk my camera to a focus that brought the lens within six feet of her, as she entered or left her nest. I cut my way to her through a thicket at such an angle that I pictured her broadside, including a full sweep of her back from the curve of her beak to the utmost tip of her long, graceful tail, in her eyes the calm, meditative, reasonable expression that always rests on the face of a cuckoo under natural conditions. I achieved the triumph of stroking this bird's wing without driving her from her nest, after having made her picture. Then I urged her by a slight push on her wing, to leave the nest that I might reproduce her eggs. I was very sorry the instant she went, because a nestling was just struggling through the shell, which explained her conduct. I had approached her at the psychological moment when the brooding fever bound her in its strongest hold. Hastily gathering up my camera and other paraphernalia, I hurriedly slipped away, but remained where I could see the nest, to which she returned almost at once, so no real damage was done.

One picture that I especially prize in my field work is that of a king rail turning and tucking an egg from sight among the feathers of her breast. In order to secure studies of this bird, it was necessary to don waist-waders and enter a swamp, where I stood much above knee-deep in muck and water while I established sufficient intimacy with her to allow me to open the grass of her nest wide enough for an exposure from beak to tail. I have several pictures of her in which she appears to be very placidly brooding without the least fear; but the first time I approached her to open her nest, with her long sharp beak she peppered my bare arms, where I had rolled my sleeves to my elbows to keep them dry while cutting grass under water, until she broke the skin to bleeding in more than a dozen places on each arm.

I highly prize the picture of a barn owl with her back toward the camera, and her head turned over her shoulder looking toward the lens, as she entered her nest.

Another prime favorite of mine is a study of a brooding male indigo finch, showing an injury to one of his eyes, undoubtedly received during a former nesting period in a thorn bush.

A picture I greatly appreciate is of a male goldfinch feeding his young. This was the first goldfinch nest I ever found that I could work on with comfort from the ground. The four youngsters filled it almost to overflowing, and from its location at the base of a levee beside the river, I had light on it for only a part of the forenoon. At this nest I secured a picture of the male bird clinging to the largest branch, from the intersection which held the structure, his side toward the camera so that the picture showed his folded wing and tail, one foot, his head, his eyes, and parted beak sharply cut, holding a morsel of food, white in color, which he was in the act of regurgitating to drop into one of the four open, upturned beaks in the cradle. This nest also showed the rain of excrement dropped over its edges by the young, for goldfinches are among the birds that do not pay any attention to this feature of parenthood.

In another location I once made a good reproduction of a brooding mother goldfinch standing on the edge of her nest turning her eggs before she entered it to brood. In all my field work I have secured such a study but twice.

When it comes to the question of temperament, I have many pictures of different kinds of hawks and a number of other birds which portray a look of calm and intelligence that is very wonderful to me. Chief among these stands a picture of a pair of dusky falcons, which I used in the illustration of "Birds of the Bible." There is also a hawk picture with a very wonderful expression of power and calm on the face of the bird, among the illustrations of that book.

At other times I have pictured anger very plainly to be discerned in a bird, which was really exhibiting anger over being disturbed at a feast of some fresh meat that I had wired to a limb on which I had focused a camera near its nesting place. There never was any trouble in getting all the pictures of greed I wanted on the faces of feeding birds, the vulture especially.

A few times I have pictured fear to such an extent that the bird's eyes seemed fairly to pop from its head. I have many pictures of birds either singing or uttering their tribal calls or cries of warning. I regard any picture which truly portrays a definite characteristic of any species on the face of a bird as very rare and interesting. I never gave my nesting birds any occasion to exhibit anger near their nest, nor was a nest on which I had a focus ever attacked by any other bird in such a way that I could reproduce the feeling of the owners. I have no study of a parent bird when it flies like a little fury to defend its brood, and none of a bird of either sex in mourning. The dissected eye of a bird shows lachrymal glands, so it may weep real tears at the loss of a mate or nestling. I never have been close enough to make sure of that.

Once from a blind, I saw a male bird come as close to laughter as a bird ever approaches outside the bubbly joy of song. My camera was focused on the nest of a pair of chewinks. I was hidden sixty feet away. The male came within a yard of me, food hunting, scratching like an industrious hen. A small rootlet was in his way and he pulled it with all his might. It broke suddenly and he fell over backward. He picked himself up, a most astonished expression on his face; then he laughed. So did I.

From a natural history standpoint, one picture of a young black vulture, made just before it learned to straighten its legs at the first joint and stand on its feet, contains more natural history than any other bird study I have so far succeeded in securing. This one picture shows how the young of these birds use the whole length of the first joint from the foot to the knee in walking. The feet are set flat upon the ground so that the partial webbing, the lining of the skin, and the size and sharpness of the toenails are clearly defined as is the immature wing. The bird is posed three quarters front toward the camera. The carrion sack plainly shows on the front of the breast in a flaccid pouch, while the bald round head is turned toward the right side so that the snow white down makes a perfect background to show the cutting of the upper and lower mandible, eye, ear, extremely large and prominent nostril, tough, leathery appearance of the cheeks, the rounded point of the lower mandible, the sharp overlapping hook of the upper; while his mouth is open to such an extent that the length, breadth, and peculiarly humanlike shape of the tongue are fully reproduced. I can not conceive how it would be possible to crowd more natural history into the likeness of one bird.

Because the robins were my father's favorite birds, and because they have such particularly charming dispositions and are so numerous and friendly, through all of my work I have been intrigued into making numbers of pictures of them. This was especially true in the Cabin, south, because it was surrounded by fruit trees and flowering shrubs and covered with vines of half a dozen different kinds. One robin picture I regard as particularly rare, because the exposure was made from my library table through heavy plate glass on the twenty-seventh of February. Counting on my protection and care, for several years this robin had been around the Cabin from one to two weeks earlier than any other bird of his kind could be seen or heard anywhere in the country. This year he outdid himself by appearing in February. The day the picture was taken the snow was six inches deep over the earth. The bird repeatedly flew to the back of an oak bench on the veranda, and with his feathers fluffed until he appeared twice the size of an ordinary robin he sat a long time looking into the house – sat so long, in fact, that I was able to make several time exposures of him.

Another robin picture which is unique is that of a male bird from a nest built in the parting of four quite large branches of a mulberry tree at the same Cabin. Thoughtlessly, to see how much they would use, I had provided these birds with torn strips of white cotton, over which they chattered and which they gathered so greedily that they advertised their nest to all creation. I had a ladder set up on a level with the nest a few yards away and had been making a very complete series of the home life of these birds. I noticed that both the male and female had the habit when they came to the nest with a beak full of worms for their young of feeding them in what might be considered turns, beginning with one and taking the four in order. Sometimes the food would all be gone before the fourth one got a bite. He would be so disappointed that he would stand in the nest, his beak wide open, and cry and beg so pitifully that both of the old birds sometimes resorted to the subterfuge of pretending to feed a youngster, when they had nothing to give. They would stretch to full height, draw up the neck, tuck in the beak, go through the motion of regurgitation, stick the beak down in the open mouth of the youngster, which quieted him, although I am sure he got no food. I tried a number of times and finally succeeded in getting a picture of the male bird in this position, when one of his nestlings was begging with particular insistence to be fed. I captioned this picture: "When Father Robin Regurgitates" without fully explaining the situation. I supposed that the picture would speak for itself, that everyone was familiar with the feeding habit of these very common birds, for they can be seen carrying beakfuls of worms from early spring to midsummer more frequently than any other of the birds of our country, at least in the northeastern United States. I understand that this picture has been questioned. Both the picture and its title are perfectly good natural history as they stand, as to feeding. It is quite true that robins carry worms in the beak to feed their young. It is equally true that they peck a long time at ripe fruit, which they swallow, and collect several ripe berries. These they regurgitate. They also make the pretense described above, while they regurgitate in yet another instance. After feeding the young, they empty the cloaca, swallowing the contents as they relieve each bird, and then on wing as they fly from the nest, I have seen them open their beaks and eject a stream half a yard in length.

Another picture which I prize highly is that of a male kingfisher, whose long, heavy beak from base to tip is scarred and worn into tiny pits from contact with the gravel and small stones in the clay back-wall of a gravel pit, in which he made his tunnel. I have always greatly appreciated an opportunity I had to secure a picture of a pair of young of this nest, when they were almost full-grown, fully feathered, and debating the question of taking wing, both of them sitting side by side in the door of their tunnel, wanting to go, yet afraid to spread their wings and launch themselves into the big world.

CHAPTER X – RARE PICTURES AFIELD

I AM particularly partial to a pair of wren pictures I have secured. At the time one of these was made an article had been published by a man had managed to set his name very high and whose word in ornithology carried weight with the people. He wrote concerning song birds that they delivered their songs with distended throats and beaks closed. I had only begun publishing and had small background before the public to sustain my word on any subject, but it appealed to me that if I could picture a number of birds in full tide of song I certainly could prove to the public that it was no more nearly possible for a bird to sing a loud, full note with its beak closed than it would be for a human being with closed lips; so with each nest worked upon I bent every effort toward securing a study of a male bird singing or the female uttering her tribal call. In the case of birds with long beaks, the width to which the points part is both surprising and amusing. I secured an excellent study one evening of a male wren that stopped on a little platform before his door and delivered himself of a long, effusive, bubbling song, before he went back to the business of catching small insects – not such small ones either – to feed his large family. After I began working especially for them, I soon had pictures of crows and jays calling, several singing cardinals, and enough other birds to convince anyone that birds sing with parted beaks.

Another good wren picture was made at a six-foot focus on this same platform, as the male wren emerged from his house, his beak widely parted on a globule from the cloacae of one of his young.

Another picture I always have regarded as rare was one I secured from the shelter of an old saw-mill on the shore of Burt Lake, where it narrows to the Indian River, on what is known in northern Michigan as the "Inland Route." The water of the shoreline was excellent feeding ground for every kind of aquatic bird of the locality, while the shelter of the mill afforded an unusual opportunity for work at close range. I had my camera focused on a blue heron, standing motionless, as he searched the surrounding water assiduously for small fish, frogs, or any living thing he might fancy for food. I had watched him so long that I had grown slightly careless. The movements, with which his beak shot down, then up, then the toss he gave the frog so that he caught it headfirst were so nearly instantaneous that I missed the rarest picture which might have been secured of him. The snap I got shows the frog at length in the course of slipping down the bird's long oesophagus, and while it is not the prize I might have had, I still regard it as rare, a true case of "a frog in the throat."

I have previously mentioned securing the likeness of a male kingbird, which seems to me almost, if not quite, my greatest triumph in bird portraiture from both scientific and artistic standpoints. The birds of this nest were so very confiding and their location was such that I could work around it with great ease and no inconvenience whatever to the birds. Among a series of two or three dozen exposures made of these birds, there was one in which the nest was sharply defined; each of the heads of the four nestlings was well outlined. The mother bird perched with her breast at about a three quarters angle toward the camera. The exposure was made just at the instant when she was regurgitating food for her young. The cutting of her beak, her eyes, her crest, and the entire detail of the picture were so fine that for scientific and artistic reasons, I regard it as very good indeed.

Twice in my life I have succeeded in photographing a brooding dove. One of these pictures was made of a bird nesting on some debris that floods had heaped on the river bank. I approached the dove by degrees with extreme caution and succeeded in setting up my camera and taking a picture of her the very first time I visited her nest. It was not a good picture. The bird's back was turned directly toward the lens and there were pieces of board and sticks that stuck up in the foreground so that they were out of focus. I worked with the lens between the spacings of a wire fence. The only way to remove the obstructions was to climb the fence and approach to within two or three feet of the bird. I did not feel that she would endure this on first acquaintance, so I made a preliminary exposure too late in the afternoon for a really good picture and went away congratulating myself upon what interesting work I should do in the morning. When morning came I found that the bird had been bound to her nest the afternoon before by the appearance of one or both of her young. As they were safely delivered from the shells and she had brooded over them all night and possibly fed them several times before my arrival, the spell was so broken that she went tearing from her nest like a mad creature while I was still several rods away. On my return from this nest, I had an encounter with a cross mare nervous over a colt barely able to walk. This was one of my most threatening and dangerous experiences afield.

In an orchard adjoining the meadow stood a decayed old apple tree having a flat piece of weather-beaten apple wood, which boys had undoubtedly thrown among the branches to knock down fruit, lodged on a low limb. The piece was wedged at one end between two branches, lay straight on a horizontal limb, the other end fitted against a good-sized twig. The concave side was up. On one end of this insecure platform, the doves had heaped a few coarse sticks and twigs for a nest, in which the mother bird was now brooding. The nest was so low that I could locate it on my finder by extending my tallest tripod full length and standing on a box about eighteen inches high to operate the camera. I secured of this bird my only pictures of a brooding dove, with the exception of the mediocre one just described. This bird brooded sidewise to the lens so that the line from the tip of her beak to the tip of her tail was unbroken. I began several rods away, but she soon told me that I could come into her location, set up my camera, take her picture, and go away. I could not move the camera a few feet closer by walking it forward on the tripod legs, as I constantly did with other birds. She would not endure having the camera move one inch toward her. As each approach gave me a more beautiful picture of her, I kept working closer, perhaps two or three feet at a time, but for every exposure, I was forced to take down the camera and tripod, carry them away, and remain awhile. Then, I could go back, approach the nest a few feet closer, and repeat the performance. Doves are universally lauded for their gentle, loving characteristics. They have a habit of searching the open roads for grain dribbling from passing wagons and the undigested corn in horse and cattle droppings, of waiting to fly until they are almost under passing wheels, settling a few seconds on fences, and at once returning to the road. These proceedings lead people into believing that doves are very tame and friendly. I never have worked around the nest of a shyer, wilder bird than a brooding dove. A male dove I never have had in range of a camera during all of my work afield, and only two different females among many I have tried for. I finally secured a picture of this orchard dove which filled a seven by nine plate, at slightly less than ten feet; but in all of my experience afield, no bird has made me exercise more patience or work harder than this bird, brooding in plain sight in an old orchard.

Another picture, which I regard as rare for its artistic as well as its scientific value, is one of a long pictorial reproduction of the history of a cowbird that invaded the river bank in my territory. This bird laid her first egg in the nest of a song sparrow, which the sparrow had just completed, but in which she had not yet deposited her first egg. The sparrow obviated the difficulty by carrying material and burying the cowbird egg, building a new floor completely over it, and raising the walls slightly higher. The next cowbird egg went into the nest of a vireo a few rods farther down the bank. I made a picture of this nest, containing two vireo eggs and one of the cowbird's. I was forced to remove one of the vireo eggs, because the cowbird had broken it, when dropping her own in the nest, while she had eaten one to make room for hers. Two more cowbird eggs were found in the nest of a black masked warbler, about the same distance from the vireo nest that it had been from the sparrow's. This nest we decided to leave untouched so that we might make a record of what would happen there. I had supposed that these four eggs would account for the cowbird's efforts in this direction, but the following morning Mr. Black and I saw her leave a thicket across the river and start down the bank in a perfect frenzy of exultation. No hen of the barnyard ever cackled and fussed over her first egg as this cowbird exulted over the successful placing of the last.

A picture which I regard as one of the most beautiful and rarest of my experience afield was made when the cowbirds were old enough to leave the nest of the warbler. The nest was built in a scraggy, little wild plum bush, the structure of dainty architecture as is the custom with warblers. By the time the cowbirds were ready to leave the nest, all of the warblers had been starved and trampled to death save one. This was a hungry little creature that from continuous fasting had put all its strength in feathers. I never have seen a young bird so curiously feathered; its plumage seemed to curl. I have seen several young chickens that had eaten something that made them sick, develop an abnormal amount of curly feathers afterward. The warbler's eyes were drawn into its head, its beak pale, and its feet scarcely had the strength to hold it; its body seemed a little pinch of bone with no flesh on it, but feathers enough for two young birds. Each of the cowbirds was easily three times the warbler's size, and five times its weight, both of them having crops so distended with food that it seemed as if they would burst, for they stood in the nest obscuring the young warbler, and with beaks wide open vociferously called for food all day long. The old warblers flew around frantically trying to still their hunger cries. As I reproduced this picture the first cowbird to abandon the nest was left where he placed himself; I helped the baby warbler to a position above, halfway between him and the nest; and the other cowbird remained in the nest during the exposure. Being sure that I had a good exposure on this rare and unusual spectacle, the young warbler was left in full possession of its home, where it is to be hoped that it finally succeeded in getting a full crop.

Among the pictures of birds uttering their cries or singing, I once secured one of a male jay near his nest, when he was crying: "Ge-rullup, ge-rullup, ge-rullup!" This bird's back was toward the camera so that the markings of his shoulders, wings, and tail showed very plainly. The back of his head and his crest were well defined; his position brought his left eye in outline; while between his open mandibles the position of his tongue in uttering his cry could be seen.

Two other jay pictures which I prize very highly for sentimental reasons are a pair of studies of a mother bird more closely paralleling human processes than any other bird picture which it has been my lot to secure or to see among the pictures of other field workers. I had a clear view of this nest. The bird was unusually beautiful. She persisted in brooding, with a calm and tranquil expression, even when the camera approached her to within less than ten feet. While I watched her from a blind at the end of sixty feet of hose one day, one of her young thrust its bare little head between the feathers of her breast, resting its chin on the edge of the nest; and in this position it went to sleep and so remained for some timelong enough at least that I had made the exposure, changed the plates, and returned to my position, before it lifted its head, opened its beak, and asked to be fed. This position I also secured.

Another favorite study of mine is almost a perfect likeness of five young shrikes. I can not claim that there is anything particularly rare from a scientific standpoint in a study of young birds, which have been handled, taken from and returned to their nest until they will allow themselves to be placed in any position; but certainly, rarely beautiful pictures with wonderful art value may be obtained in this way. These proceedings result in no harm whatever to the birds as I never have failed to return to a nest, and have it remain, any young bird that I handled for pictorial purposes. I was particularly happy in the selection of a perch for these young birds, for just at the time it was needed I was able to find a maple branch having two nearly parallel limbs small enough for the young birds to perch upon without an appearance of discomfort or awkwardness. I made several studies of them before returning them to their nest and their parents. In the best of these the oldest and youngest nestlings were placed for contrast upon the top limb, the oldest one in a clean-cut profile, the baby face front. On the limb below were the three intermediate birds, the one to the left breast front with his head turned so that his beak is in profile, the middle one with his back toward the lens, his head sufficiently turned to give a good view of the beak and eye, and the one on the right perched in profile giving a different view of his head, beak, and eye. The limbs were covered with lichens, which so harmonized with the feathering of the young birds that it made of them almost perfect examples of protective coloration. Added to all of the care used in posing these birds, it must be noted that all birdland does not contain nestlings surpassing them in beauty or interest. In family, they are near enough the hawk tribe to have big, liquid eyes, curved beaks, and the appearance of wisdom and poise, while their soft feathering is so spineless that it is like down of a dim grey color, faintly peppered with darker touches almost invisible, the wing and tail feathers at their first appearance being sharply touched with patches of black and white.

While on the subject of young birds, which I have reproduced by the hundreds, there come to my mind preeminently half a dozen pictures of a pair of young kingfishers which I had taken from their nest, handled, and returned so often that they would remain in any position in which I placed them. Two pictures of these young ones are particularly good. To these I might add the likeness of a pair of young cuckoos, which never fail to bring a cry of delight to the lips of anyone to whom I show them. I have also one study of a pair of young cardinals, male and female, which is conspicuous among dozens of the kind.

From a perching hummingbird on a la France rose I secured an unusual study of this bird of humming, tireless wing; while quail once gave me an excellent example of protective coloration, as have killdeers, larks, and bitterns in the Wabash River. I have no brooding study of which I am prouder than that of a hen lark, which entered her nest, after I had opened it slightly wider than she had designed it, and before a hidden lens settled herself to brooding at an angle which gave a long sweep from tip to tail, her head and eyes beautifully outlined, her head and back coloring almost indistinguishable from her nest. A careless observer might have looked straight at her and never seen either the bird or her nest. Her position in brooding hid her neck and breast decorations. Among my rare robin studies I should have mentioned one of a mother bird standing her feathers on end, just as she stepped into her nest to hover her brood, so that the young might lay their heads against the warmth of her bare breast. This study is the only one of its kind I have secured or have seen.

I always have-been particularly pleased over the picture of a hen calling a flock of fluffy little chickens, twenty in number, to the shelter of her wings, a study for which I worked long and hard to illustrate the Biblical passage: "like as a hen gathereth her chickens."

After much experience with pigeons in cotes extending the length of an old barn on a back lot at Limberlost Cabin, south, I succeeded in securing only one picture of a male kissing his mate.

I always shall regard the pictures of the drunken waxwing, discussed in a previous chapter, as extremely unique and of much interest.

Among studies of birds uttering their tribal calls, I have one very fine and characteristic crow picture, and I also have a unique study of a crow stealing a lens. I secured this by placing the lens with its shining brass rim in a conspicuous place on a log, focusing and covering a set camera, and hiding in a blind at a distance until the bird was tempted, as I hoped it would be, to pick up the lens. Almost simultaneously I was forced to hurl a stick at the bird in order to make it drop the lens, which was a fine rectilinear nearly two inches in diameter.

CHAPTER XI - LEARNING BIRD LANGUAGE

IN STUDYING the birds in their native haunts it is the greatest help imaginable to know their language and to be able to recognize their voices. The first thing to learn is the tribal call of each species, that note which in its most frequent utterance on the part of the female is the simple question: "Where?" and on the part of the male the reply: "Here." This question is repeatedly asked and answered by all birds, even before and after the brooding season, when they are pleasuring or food hunting through the fields and forests. It is the out-cropping of the love of company, a feeling ingrained in the hearts of birds and beasts, as of men. It is a direct result of the dread of being alone, a love of friends, a wish to know if kindred are near. So at this quick, inquiring call, usually of one note, wren answers wren, robin calls to robin, jay replies to jay.

After courting is over and a pair is nest building, this call comes with greater frequency, since the strongest tie existing between birds has just been formed, they being paired in some instances for several matings, frequently for life. During incubation it is scarcely heard from the female except in time of alarm, as its utterance would attract attention to the nest location. When the young are hatched and both the elders are busy gathering food a period of greatest anxiety ensues, and the call and answer pass between the parents with almost clock-like regularity. This serves the double purpose of letting the pair know of the safety of each other and the young that they have not been deserted.

In no case in my experience with the birds have I ever heard this call given with such frequency and precision as by a pair of chewinks. For two days before the young left the nest, my camera was focused on their location. The old birds went before it from the first, without the slightest hesitation. There was a long hose attached; I was hidden in a near-by thicket. As a protection from swarms of mosquitoes, I covered myself with a long cravenette, matching the shade of the dead leaves under foot, so that it concealed me entirely and fitted into the surroundings perfectly. Those birds hunted altogether on the ground; their use of the tribal call was regular and frequent. Four and five times to the minute, by my watch, came the question of the female: "Che-wink?" and the immediate answer of the male: "Che-wee."

If for any reason the male was slow in answering, a change could be detected instantly in the tone of the female. Her call was a degree sharper, tinctured with a faint hint of anxiety. If the male still failed to answer, she immediately flew to the region of the nest and called again, this time a call so filled with anxiety and excitement that it constituted an alarm cry. So they talked every minute of the time I worked around them. The case is similar with almost any bird of bubbling song of which I can think. Brown thrashers and cuckoos are quieter.

With most sparrows and finches, the call is, "Chip," with cardinals the male calls, "Chip" and the female frequently answers, "Chook." The male robin calls, "Kip," and the female answers, "Cut." Both quail use the same call, "Chet." With doves the call and answer are "Coo." Wood thrushes call, "Pit," and wood-peckers, "Kerr." Crows call, "Caw;" king rails, "Gyck;" and shitepokes, "Couk."

Some birds utter an elliptical call that can be expressed only by the use of an apostrophe. Blue jays have the same call and answer, "D'jay;" kingbirds, "T'sheup;" blackbirds, "T'check;" skylarks, "Z'sst."

With a large class, the call has two clearly defined syllables. Blue herons call, "Ker-awk." Both catbirds call, "Me-ow," and often, "Ma-a-ry! Ma-a-ry!" Killdeers say, "Te-dit," and bluebirds call, "Su-gar." These tribal calls are used ordinarily as a method of ascertaining the location of a pair, and to assure each other that all is well.

The danger signal is nothing more than the tribal call repeated in a quicker time, touched with anxiety and raised in tone. If the danger is great and immediate these tones are intensified and the call almost invariably repeated, three times, at least among small birds. In case their nest is invaded or they are taken rudely in hand they utter a shrill, prolonged scream and defend themselves by scratching and picking when possible. Among big birds like the blue heron the cry is simply prolonged and rasping in proportion to the size of the bird. A heron can be heard nearly a mile on land and farther across water.

About the business of living, a hawk utters a high, weird cry, but in case of actual battle all members of the family, whenever possible, lie on the back and present a formidable array of claws and beak, hissing, as is the habit of an angry gander.

Owls are extremely noisy in their first hunting after much early winter sleeping. Ours become active the latter part of January unless the cold is extreme. Until the females begin brooding the great horned owls of the Cabin, north, hunt in pairs, crying regularly to each other. Either of the pair selects a favorable shelter for small birds and with spread wings flies into it with full force, crying: "Wack, wack, wack!" in guttural tones. In case prey is flushed, the pair joins forces, both crying excitedly and both sinking their claws into the same bird, rabbit, or groundhog. Often they carry prey to the roof of the Cabin and pitiful screams of a rabbit are added to the birds' excited pandemonium. The still higher, prolonged, wildcat or panther scream of the great horned owl is infrequent, uttered, many think, to scare up prey or to paralyze with fright some creature that has been sighted, but I am not sure. This would seem to be the reasonable explanation of it, but every time I have heard it the scream was uttered from high locations and in such a manner that I thought its most probable intent was to breed fear in the forest, to say to all living things that a frightful creature was abroad; therefore it would be highly proper to quake and tremble. I really think this owl scream is uttered with the same intent as the challenging roar of a full-fed lion, secure in his strength, out seeking trouble. I interpret it: "I am here in my might! Come on, if you dare!"

Danger signals are always heeded by the birds, in no case of the wild more intuitively than by barnyard fowl, which use a prolonged scream. When a little girl, I peeped with breathless interest over my mother's shoulder while she removed newly hatched chickens from under a brooding hen in the fear that the hen would think all of her family had emerged and leave her nest too soon. As my mother lifted the hen to see if she had found all of the chickens, a tiny, triangular piece of shell flew up on an egg.

"There!" said Mother, "that is the beginning. The little chicken has broken the shell with its bill; now it will soon be out."

"Oh, Mother!" I begged, "do please let me take it. Let me hold it in my hand when it comes out!" My mother picked up the egg, laid it in my hand, while I stood with my back to the wind, carefully cupping my other hand over the shell, issuing a series of bulletins: "There goes another big piece!" "It's struggling hard now!" "There goes an awful big piece!" "It will be out in a minute!" Near us an old rooster uttered that prolonged scream which means: "Hawk coming! Hide for your lives!" that danger signal which sends every hen in the barnyard to cover with her brood. Turkey hens crouch in the tall grass, sometimes even gobblers hide, while guineas dart under the fences. As a rule turkey gobblers and ganders stand on defense, ready to fight.

"That settles it!" exclaimed my mother, carefully replacing the egg. "That chicken will not move again for half an hour, and I can not possibly spare that much time." When I read in the writings of Darwin that an unhatched chicken that had neither breathed nor seen light would lie dormant for a long period, at the danger signal of a cock, I instantly remembered this experience of my childhood, and wondered where my mother learned it; yet, things like this which my parents taught me always have proved true afield.

The tribal call once repeated, raised, and intensified to a scream of rage, is the battle cry of the birds, and comes when they attack a rival, a crow around a nest, a cat, a squirrel, or a human being.

The same cry, in greater agony and prolonged, comes when a bird is wounded, caught in a trap or by a cat, or when its young are being taken from the nest by strangers. This cry is commonly described as a "squall" or "squawk."

A large number of songbirds have one song of greater or less length, which is sung in differing ways in different circumstances. Of course, the imitators such as catbirds, brown thrashers, and mocking birds change their song in imitation of whatever sounds they hear while singing or remember from former songs. But most of the others sing a succession of notes in individual ways, while some improvise as they sing, like the bobolink.

In the early spring, after the disbanding of families for the season, and through the winter, the song of the birds is one of joyful abandon. When they are full-fed, free, content, the music bubbles from their throats in a swelling chorus. Sometimes they sing their notes at the highest pitch they can reach, then in middle tone, and then with scarcely parted beak they warble them over in a greatly distended throat, diminishing to a mere whisper of sound, which they sometimes continue for the full length of their strain. The black-headed grosbeak is probably master of this art, but in much experience in study of the songs male birds sing, while I am hidden with a camera near the mate to which they sing, I have learned that this is much more common among birds than is generally known. Almost all of them sing whisper songs that must be for their own pleasure.

Sometimes bird song is trailed over the fields, beside the river, and through the woods, interspersed with snatches of food and playful darts after other birds. But when really singing and enjoying their own performance, the beak is pointed upward to a greater or less degree – greater among very small birds – the throat swells, the feathers of the breast and back ruffle over the wings so that the impression is formed that the wings are pressed tightly to the sides; the tail is folded and bends under the body slightly, and the beak parts narrowly in some species, widely in others.

The song of all songs is the passion song. In this the males make their supreme effort. It begins when the mating fever attacks them, intensifies in pursuit of a mate, and reaches the acme, the fullest force and expression, immediately prior to the act of mating. The catbird then surpasses himself; the wood thrush, hermit thrush, and brown thrasher out-sing their sweetest performances; the oriole flames in voice as in body; and the chewink is an insistent and irresistible wooer. But I know of no other bird that in the stress of mating fever, so swells, prolongs, and trills his notes, so spreads and rocks himself, and displays his charms, as the cardinal grosbeak. With feathers upstanding on breast and back until his wings are almost obscured, with swollen throat, crest flared to the utmost, and parted beak, he begins; and as he approaches and reaches the greatest degree of intensity, he sways, his wings half lifted and half spread, and whistles and trills and tumbles out his notes in a frenzy. Although not generally conceded, it is a fact that nearly every female sings a number of times a day, during courtship and feeding, never when brooding, except the merest whisper. These songs suggest the notes of the male, but they are low, hesitating, uttered in such a way that they do not compare favorably with the efforts of the master musician.

When you see a bird about the daily business of life, suddenly stop, plaster its feathers to its body, and its eyes snap and pop, it is so paralyzed with fear that until it has a second in which to recover it can not decide in which direction to fly. And very frequently birds save their lives when overtaken by imminent danger by flattening their feathers, remaining where they are, and trusting to protective coloring to hide them.

When a bird flares its crest, or lacking a crest raises its crown feathers, lifts its wings from its body, leans forward, and peers from side to side, it is inquisitive, not really frightened; but it has discovered something sufficiently out of the ordinary to awaken its interest. In such case, if nothing happens to cause it to take flight, it usually begins talking and soon calls up all the feathered folk within hearing to help decide what interests it. Frequently in case of flight the bird reconsiders and cautiously approaches at times very near the object which first alarmed it. Some birds are much more curious than others. A wren or a vireo among small birds, or a catbird or a jay among larger ones, can assemble the whole wood to investigate a camera, which, until their attention was called to it, the other birds were passing with indifference. My father used to say that more wild turkeys fell victim to their own curiosity than to the snares and traps of men. Wild and domestic animals have a manifest propensity to run from an object that frightens them at first sight, then reconsider, return to investigate, and frequently the wild animals, through curiosity, enter a trap from which the first impulse was to run.

Once as I lay tired out in the bottom of a boat on the Wabash, a tiny red-eyed vireo came peeking and peering, softly repeating to himself: "Du, du, du!" Nothing happened, so he ventured closer, until he was on a twig not a yard from my face. "Peai?" he began asking. "Peai?" No response or motion was made, so he ventured even nearer, raised his voice, and bravely screamed, "Tishvon! Tishvoo!" at me, until he awakened the woods. The birds of all kinds came flocking from all directions, and, following the example of the vireo, drew close to investigate. I was having one of those rare treats which at times fall to the lot of a field worker, when a drove of pigs came near, and to keep them from becoming entangled in the hose attached to my best camera I was compelled to move. The investigating committee hastily dispersed in every direction.

The expression of greed flashes instantaneously into the eyes of a crow, hawk, or vulture when the bird is discovered at a feast particularly to its liking. Birds prove that they are greedy by risking their lives to remain with food they are eating, by almost choking themselves and at times their young by trying to force down bites too large for their throats. Sometimes they raise the head high, twist, stretch, and turn the neck to force down an especially large fragment.

Action, voice, and expression combine when birds are angry. Usually the plumage is raised in the scream of anger, and then more swiftly contracts with action, as they make the plunge which carries them to their foe.

Some of the larger birds, the eagle, hawk, and vulture, speak a plain language of defiance. With sleek feathers and flashing eyes, they part their beaks and utter a hiss which means: "I will fight before you shall touch my young."

Last of all, and hardest to learn, and with no way of understanding just how or why it happens, you can study the language of intuition among the birds. You can see that in some way you can not fathom, a whole flock, perching on a tree, feeding on the ground, or drinking at the river, can become alarmed as one bird, rise with one accord, and fly for their lives. Sometimes, by careful watching, you can see a man coming with a gun, a snake crossing the river, or a weasel slipping under a log; and sometimes, try as you may, you can in no way discover the cause of alarm. It is the same impulse of fear that at times sets herds of cattle and horses in motion, or drives a large body of men to panic.

Hunters and woodsmen depend greatly on the birds for news of the forest. Sometimes a catbird or a jay discovers their presence and alarms their game; but to repay that, the birds often tell men that game is approaching. A bird especially disliked among duck hunters is the godwit. It is a regular alarm clock, while other ducks heed its warnings every time, to the great disgust of hunters hidden in blinds, or shooting over decoys.

By a careful study of bird calls, cries, and notes, any good imitator can talk with more birds than one would imagine possible. I know a man who can toll an oriole across an orchard, and another who can bring a lark across a meadow. My husband taught my parrot a perfect "Bob White" call. One day there was a knock at the door and when I opened it a man said: "There is a quail among your rose bushes. My wife is ill, and if you don't mind I'd like to get it mighty well."

I asked him to step inside, and showed him the "quail" he wanted to shoot. He surely was surprised.

Unfortunately, my mouth is so very large and my tongue so contrary I can not whistle, so my repertoire is very limited. I learned the screech owl call, practicing a poem. I tried it on an owl and got an answer. By accident I learned that I could call a goldfinch. I was washing negatives in the kitchen sink. The back door was open. In the backyard grew a forest of sunflowers for the parrot's winter food, and over them the goldfinches hovered constantly. As I worked, I kept repeating the goldfinch call to perfect myself in it.

I did my very best, and to my astonishment, from the yard came a male goldfinch's answer, "P'tsee me?" Instantly I changed to the female cry,

"P'tseet!" The goldfinch answered from the sweet pea rack. I hid behind the door, and watched through the crack.

"P'tsee me?"

"P'tseet!"

The goldfinch was on the walk.

"P'tsee me?"

"P'tseet!"

The goldfinch was on the paper barrel beside the steps.

"P'tsee me?"

"P'tseet!"

The goldfinch was on the back porch.

"P'tsee me?"

"P'tseet!"

The goldfinch was at the screen door, hopping back and forth to find an entrance, and had the door been open undoubtedly I could have called him inside. Since then I talk with these birds whenever I choose, having ample opportunity; for they are always with us from June until November.

I learned the tribal call of the king rail in the hope of locating him in a swamp, so that I could find and picture his young; but while I could win a reply easily enough, I never could get near enough to secure anything save an effect of snakes in the grass, as he darted among the rushes.

That I could speak shitepoke with sufficient fluency to get a reply, I also learned by accident. I was driving east of the Cabin, south, with a helper, over the levee which crosses the Valley of the Wood Robin, on a trip to the old Aspy orchard. A shitepoke flew up south of us, crossed the road before us, and perched in a scraggy, dead top limb of a big sycamore north of the road.

"That is a shitepoke, isn't it?" asked the lad.

"It is," I answered.

"What does it say?" questioned the boy, who was a lover of birds and one of my most ardent helpers.

"Couk, couk, couk!" I answered.

"Couk, couk, couk!" instantly replied the shitepoke.

In amazement, we stared at each other. He slackened the horse to a walk, whispering: "Call again!"

I turned, stood on my knees on the seat, and, shielded by the raised carriage top, cupped my hands around my mouth and did my best. The bird replied immediately. I waited a second and called with greater caution, with accent and inflection nearer the bird's own than before. Instantly the shitepoke gave a cry and spreading its wings flew to the road, where it followed three rods in our direction before it realized that the call was coming from the carriage. Since then I talk with the shitepokes and call them across the valley whenever I choose.

There is nothing to prevent anyone from talking with those birds whose tribal calls can be imitated with the voice, and a throaty or half-whispered nasal utterance. A commotion can always be raised in the woods by hiding in a bird neighborhood and uttering a series of judiciously spaced and intoned screech owl calls. A large number of birds will answer a call that can be made by placing the lips on the back of the hand, and producing a sharp, loud, indrawn, kissing sound inflected like a chirp. A perfect brown thrasher alarm cry results, and a very good crested flycatcher's. All thrushes are interested, and catbirds. Even the domestic canaries, hatched and raised in the bird-house in my conservatory, will answer and become much agitated over this call. Slight practice is all that is required.

Anyone who is an expert whistler can soon combine vocal and whistled calls, so that he can depend on a reply from almost any bird he attempts to imitate. The instant he receives a response, comes the feeling that the bird is his, and a closer tie than ever before existed is established. This possessive feeling comes only through knowledge acquired by personal contact with the birds. The bird that you can teach to bear your presence about its young arouses a warmer feeling than you ever have had for any other of its kind, while the bird which will talk with you is a friend indeed.

CHAPTER XII - WHAT BIRDS SAY AND SING

"NOW, after the 'flight of ages,' when the birds had emerged from the state of monstrosity, each raw singer having chanted continuously his individual tonic, there came a time when they must take a long step forward and enter the world of song. In the vast multitude of feathered creatures there must have been an endless variety of forms and sizes, and a proportionate variety in the pitch and quality of their voices. Day to day, year to year, each bird had heard his fellows squall, squawk, screech, or scream their individual tones, till in due time he detected here and there in the tremendous chorus certain tones that had a special affinity for his own. This affinity, strengthened by endless repetitions, at last made an exchange of tones natural and easy. Suppose there were two leading performers the key of one being G, and the key of the other being D, a fifth above G, what could have been more natural than for these two voices to unite, either on D, or G, or both, and to vibrate into one? This accomplished, the bondage of monotony and chaos was broken forever, and progress assured; the first strain of the marvelous harmony of the future was sounded, the song of the birds was begun. One can almost hear those rude, rising geniuses exercising their voices with increased fervor, vibrating from one to five and five to one of the scale-pushing on up the glad way of liberty and melody. With each vibration from one to five and from five to one, the leading tone of the scale, the other member of the common chord, which so affinitizes with one and five, was passed over. The next step was to insert this tone, which being done, the employment of the remaining tones was simply a matter of time. So it was, to my notion, that the birds learned to sing."SIMEON PEASE CHENEY.

The song of some of the birds at its present state of evolution is such a rolling jumble of sound that I never have heard any scientist or musician attempt to translate it into our language – even in the crudest form of syllables – or to set it in notes on the musical staff. The best example of this kind of music is that of the common house wren. He is an indefatigable singer, yet no one has ever tried to syllabify or register his notes on the staff, to my knowledge. I doubt gravely if anyone ever will. The wren is such a rollicking, bubbling, little whiff of spontaneity, feathers, and bones that his jumbled notes are hopeless of reproduction. He sings constantly around nesting locations, aggressively during his courting season, endlessly while at the joyous task of rearing his brood. He sings while industriously searching fruit trees for slugs, bugs, and spiders; he sings past a beak crammed full of worms and insects; he sings during heavy downpours of rain; he sings in any location, under any condition, during the entire time he remains with us. When he leaves his nesting location, having his brood successfully reared, and goes to the seclusion of the woods to moult, when other birds are shy, wild, and for the most part invisible, one still hears the notes of the wren; and this is quite remarkable, for other song birds are almost voiceless when moulting, sluggish of flight, and appear as if they enjoy life less than at any other time. Dressed in his new coat, for a week or ten days before his winter tour to the South he returns to the haunts of spring, and sings almost as continuously as he did at that time. His call note is a wiry wisp of sound, no more reproducible than his song. In case his nest and young are interfered with he is a valiant little fighter, but what he says can be described no better than as angry chatter. He is profane on provocation, and, pushed to the limit, swears like the proverbial sailor. He does not hesitate to make physical attack on anyone disturbing his nest or mate, flying like a small fury at the head and eyes of a human, who must appear bigger to a wren than an elephant does to us.

No bird of our ornithology is more beloved in the North than the bluebird. In company with the martin or sometimes a day or two before or very shortly after, the bluebird is one of the first to put in an appearance in the earliest spring. Poets have written much concerning the gorgeous blue of his back, the sweet, friendly twitter of his homecoming, the cheerfulness of his disposition, but no one has very much to say concerning his song. The first we hear of the bluebird in the spring is a long-drawn, melodiously inflected call note: "Sugar! Sugar!" often accompanied, especially around a bird-box, with a flutter of wings, which might truly be described as a combination of sound and feathers. His song falls into the same measure as the robin's, but it is very different in cadence. The robin selects a choir loft, looks around him to make sure that he has at least a feathered audience, while very frequently he seeks a human one; then he throws up his head, parts his beak widely, and rolls forth the notes with vast assurance. The bluebird has a timid, deprecatory manner, and always to me there is a plaintive tone. When his life history with us is taken into consideration, this is not much of a marvel; for in my experience, bluebirds come to grief ten times to a robin's once. The bluebird arrives so early in March, coming sometimes even as early as February, that he faces cold, ice and storm, spring gale, heavy downpour, and scarcity of food. Frequently a pair lose their nest, because they love to build in bird-houses placed for them. These houses very frequently are set with poor judgment, so that they are constantly preyed upon by cats and red squirrels; while it is impossible so to construct bird-boxes that they will admit a bluebird and exclude its bitterest enemy, the English sparrow. Very frequently, bluebirds bring off two or three broods to the season; so I fee- justified by the facts in stating that this singer has a touch of melancholy in his voice, while I am surely right in attributing to him only minor notes. He has a placid face and appealing character, because he keeps on singing even when his nest has been destroyed repeatedly. As nearly as the song can be put into syllables, it is best translated: "Pu-ri-ty, pu-ri-ty, pu-ri-ty!" with plenty of quaver and not much height or depth of tone.

The bird of our dooryard and orchard, best known of all and probably best loved, is the robin. His tribal call is: "Kip, kip!" and he speaks loudly and plainly when he says it, often as if he desired to attract human attention. This I think he does undoubtedly, since from the beginning of homes in America he has been a bird protected and loved more than any other throughout the North. There are occasions when he has been shot on the grounds that he ate too many cherries, but for one person of my experience who has shot robins, I could name a small host who would be more inclined to shoot the person who shot the bird, than to do the robin any damage. I have been told that in the South, especially in Texas, the robin multiplies in great numbers and becomes intoxicated on fermenting fruit so that his appearance is that of a bedraggled toper, and his manners decidedly questionable; but with this phase of his life I am not acquainted. There is no bird song dearer to my heart – not even that of the inimitable wood thrush. Of course, the wood thrush far surpasses the robin in melody, but until building the Cabin, north, I have been compelled to follow this thrush to the woods – even to the deep woods – and efface myself completely, often in most unpleasant places, in order to hear his notes. All day, busy with the affairs of life, from basement to garret of any home I ever lived in, I have heard the robin singing most exquisitely, as plainly as anything I ever said myself, the tender words: "Cheer up, dearie, cheer up, dearie, cheer up, cheer up, cheer!" Frequently during the heaviest field work of May and June I have come back to the Cabin at the point of exhaustion from one of my hardest days afield with burning, blistered shoulders, aching feet, and tired eyes, for we often have extreme heat in late June; and I have gotten a fresh grip on life and my work from the robin's melodious and infectious admonitions of cheer. From a musical standpoint it is an excellent song that he sings, with a clear, melodious beginning, well sustained notes, and pleasing ending. I am particularly fond of a bird that ends his song. After experiencing the suspense of waiting for an oriole to complete his strain, I feel particularly thankful to a robin for coming to a happy, definite ending. Robins of several seasons enlarge their repertoire with lovely notes, learned from their closest neighbours, the orioles, song sparrows, and bluebirds. I often hear my robins dropping in these notes at random in their song.

Another household pet, a part of the family life at the Cabin, is the chickadee. His call note is given in the freest manner, with the most human inflection of any bird note I know. The little whiff of grey feathers, sharply touched with black and white, comes fluttering around the back door for crumbs, conversationally remarking: "Chick-a-dee-dee-dee!" Sometimes he leaves off the first two syllables and simply says: "Dee, dee, dee!" His song is two or three pure sweet whistled notes that I can not reproduce in words, and can not find reproduced in any book on bird music in my library. He is a winter bird that takes the summer place of the wrens around the Cabin, even tamer than the wrens; for with a few minutes of immovable offering of food, when the chickadee is cold and hungry in winter, he can be induced to alight on the head or hands to pick at a piece of bread.

I have had as much, if not more, personal experience with the cardinal than with any other bird of our ornithology. He was a close friend of my childhood, handled constantly as a pet bird during my school days. When I went afield with a camera, I set it up before more cardinal nests than those of any other birds, because my first book dealt only with his kind; so it was necessary to have a large number of interesting reproductions of his free, wild life for the illustrations. The cardinal is a bird extremely alert, living on high nervous tension. If a bird has any idea of self-protection, it would seem that a cardinal, making a flaming target every time he wings his flight in the open, would naturally keep to the shrubbery and underbrush, but not so. Beside public highways, in all kinds of thickets and bushes on the banks of rivers, in orchards, grape vines, and gardens, he builds; and one pair, in my childhood, nested on a bough of a Norway pine only a few feet from our front door and not four feet from the ground.

With every intrusion of human, animal, or other bird, both cardinals begin to fly around excitedly, the male crying, "Chip! chip!" each note cut off in a manner extremely abrupt. In times of excitement, the female answers, "Chip!" but when she is brooding or has a nestful of young in her care, and the cry of the male bird is merely a note of inquiry, she frequently answers with a soft, throaty "Chook" that reminds me of the tones of a clucking hen. In his music, the cardinal is a whistler, and he varies his strain much more frequently than the average feathered musician. One of his famous whistled tunes is a repetition of the same notes: "Wheat, wheat, wheat!" Again, he very distinctly cries: "Here, here, here!" and like the flicker in using the same word but entirely different in the sound, he also whistles: "Wet, wet, wet!" In his more elaborate strains he very clearly whistles: "Come here" in three or four repetitions, but beginning on a lower note, rising higher, and prolonging and trilling different notes so that the song is full of sound variations. Numbers of different interpretations, equally apt, may be put upon the notes of the cardinal. Once a sweet faced old lady asked me to name the bird, which came through her orchard singing: "Pretty, pretty, pretty!" She imitated the cardinal so perfectly that I knew instantly which bird she meant. In the course of my childhood around nests and in my field experiences with a camera, I have watched the love affairs of many birds, but I know of no bird that in the ecstasy of the mating fever becomes so obsessed as the cardinal.

He is not the only musician in the family; his mate does very well on a low whistled repetition of most of his notes. In truth the hens of almost every species with which I am intimately acquainted sing a few soft, low songs during courtship, sometimes after family cares are over in the nest.

The best thing ever said about a cardinal in my experience was a remark made by Ross Lower, a small boy of Wabash, Indiana. He was standing on the sidewalk in utter absorption, listening to a thrilling courting song of a cardinal in a tree close the fence. A woman passing noticed his interest and pausing asked: "What do you think he is saying?" to which he promptly replied: "I think he says: 'Keep the home fires burning.'" I agree with the lad. That is exactly what a cardinal says in his mating song, which is his most finished utterance

The nuthatch is another resident at the Cabin, north. His tribal call is: "Yank, Yank, Yank!" He is a very free bird, coming around the Cabin frequently during the summer when he is nesting in hollow trees in the woods; but in the winter he fellowships with the chickadee, titmouse, junco, and downies, picking at the suet baskets, feasting on the store provided on the deep windowsills of the bird porch, and performing the acrobatic stunt of running headfirst down the trees. His sustained song is an elaboration of his cry. He seldom takes time to sing. When he does, his tone is low and almost human. Quite conversationally he remarks, rather than sings: "Yank! Yank! Yank-ee! Yank-ee! Yank! Yank! Yank!"

A very quiet and well conducted little member of our winter choir, with habits similar to those of the nuthatch, is the junco, with dark head and back, white breast, and grey sides. With an ivory white bill, he feasts daintily at our winter offerings, occasionally remarking: "'tsip, 'tsip." This is merely a whisper of sound. Occasionally he pauses and whistles a high, halting strain of a few notes with small variation that I am unable to give any form of syllabication.

Another extremely interesting small bird sometimes seen in the summer, but constantly with us in winter, is the titmouse. His soft, delicate plumage, his sharp crest, his bright eye, and his gaudy vest make him a beautiful creature, reminding me of the cedarbird in form. Clear and high, when food hunting around the Cabin and especially in spring, he calls: "Hewit, hewit!" very seldom repeating the words more than once, each time making them clearly words, as I should speak them; at other times he drags his utterances. His song is high, clear, and beautifully musical in the winter woods, but so nearly like the wren's in bubbling spontaneity that I again confess myself unable to put it into syllables or give it sympathetic description.

The master singer of our winter woods, with one exception the bird dearest to my heart, is the song sparrow. His call note is a clear "Chip! chip!" One of these birds homed on a small point and was nesting there, when I purchased my present location. I staked off his site, and every man of dozens of workers, spending a year in the construction of the Cabin, knew about the song sparrow's nest; while most of them tossed him crumbs from their dinner pails. Every winter he has homed with us, and at times when no other bird – not even the cardinal – lifts his voice, the song sparrow, perching on a maple down at the shore line, in bold, clear tones, has given at least a short concert in the morning during our bitterest January weather, until the extreme cold of 1918, during which I lost him. A song sparrow came to the point in the spring and nested near the old site. He is there the winter of 1919 singing each February morning as I work on this book, but he is not the master musician we had the four years previous. There is a world of difference between his halting, imperfectly pitched rendition of the song sparrow's notes and that of his loved predecessor, who was a grand opera singer, his tune gay and colorful. He always started on three short notes, sometimes preceded by a grace note quite an octave lower. He reached the last A on a piano keyboard. From that, he rose to a D above, fell back to A, dropped lower to F, rose to B, and finished with the A on which he began. As nearly as his song can be reduced to words, it runs: "Fitz, fitz, fitz, we, we-sir, sir-wee, sir-witz, witz." This syllabication may help amateurs in bird song to recognize the song sparrow notes when they hear them, but the words look so awkward in print and fall so far short of conveying my ideas of the melody of this performance that I hesitate to set them down. No bird of the sparrow or finch tribes can come anywhere near the song sparrow in improvisation. He can deliver half a dozen different variations, all based on the same strain. Every song sparrow I have heard almost invariably begins a concert with: "Fitz, fitz" on A. Several experts on bird song consider him "nature's cleverest song genius." In summer his music is not so noticeable in the Babel of warblers, finches, robins, orioles, catbirds, thrushes, and blackbirds, which pour a confusion of song around the Cabin; but in winter, when he has only chickadees, juncos, and titmice, with an occasional song of the cardinal, with which to compete, he easily holds the centre of the stage as the most continuous and melodious performer.

Dropping in among the other winter singers and at times in the summer as well, comes the metallic "Chink, chink" of the downy woodpecker. If he has any other song I am not familiar with it.

At the same time the flicker is crying: "Wet, wet, wet." One writer on bird notes translates this cry: "Quit, quit" but to my ear he very distinctly says, "Wet." He is a bird of cheery disposition, noisy and conspicuous of voice as he is of color in the winter woods. Sometimes, when drumming on a hollow tree, he lifts his head and in high, clear tones cries: "Keeyer!" It is difficult to say whether his notes are sung or whistled. There is something of the quality of both. The bird seems to vocalize them. In an attempt to reproduce them it would certainly be necessary to whistle the tones at least partially.

Among our Cabin musicians, the wailing quaver of the screech owl is heard from half a dozen different directions at the same time. The cry might be likened to a sneeze imperfectly syllabified: "T'cher-r-whieu" the last syllable drawn out and wavering until it makes you shiver at times, again it is cut off in rather short, sharp delivery.

The barred owl and the barn owl deliver a succession of: "Whoo-who-hoo, to-whoo-ah'"s their cries differently divided and inflected, but both birds uttering a succession of these syllables in different combinations. To the ear of the average human, any owl cry is harrowing, yet these owls seldom lift their voices except when they are making love or feeding, neither occupation being in the least disagreeable to humanity.

One of the component parts of life at Limberlost Cabin, north, either summer or winter is the great horned owls. We have magnificent specimens, standing over two feet in height, with a yard of wing sweep; their residence I shall not betray. For these birds I have a peculiar feeling of compassion, since the hand, the trap, and the gun of everyone else are against them. It is my business to guard their location, to dump into the lake the bodies of poisoned chickens set for them, to release them from traps, to forbid guns, and to protect them in every way possible to me; although I very well know that on summer nights they prey upon many of my most beautiful and musical song birds perching in thickets and grape vine entanglements. In a prolonged, wavering cry, the utterance of the horned owl runs: "Whoo, hoo-hoo! Whoo, hoo-hoo-hoo!" There is a time during December and early January when these birds are seldom heard, but late in January and through February, unless the winter be unusually severe, they cry almost incessantly through the woods at this their mating season; toward spring, when the young have hatched and begun to have growing appetites, the wavering cry of the owls, when food hunting, is nothing less than hair-raising. Added to this cry they have a scream, which I think many uninitiated persons have attributed to the wildcats and panthers. This cry is a hideous prolonged scream, sounding more like the voice of a wildcat than any other note I ever heard from the throat of a bird. My owls use it from a high perch with seeming intent to terrify to paralysis all woodland creatures. On wing, just as they plunge into a thicket of bushes or vines striking with full force in order to scare up sleeping birds, they cry in horrid, guttural tones: "Wack! Wack! Wack!" the pair often voicing the cries in a jumble of repellent sounds. In describing the horned owl's scream, Chapman calls it "one of the most blood-curdling sounds I have ever heard in the woods," while Schuyler Matthews says: "No cat on a backyard fence can produce a sound as hideous."

Always, summer and winter, we have with us an abundance of crows with their "Caw! caw! caw!" Listening to these notes, Morning Face, fresh from a city residence, once remarked to me: "Hark the caw-bird!" In a family discussion, which takes on a tone of dissension, in prolonged syllables there comes from the summer woods the crow cry: "Ca-cack-ca-caw!"

Like our titmouse in syllabication, but the notes raised in tone, every summer the oriole comes into my woods crying: "Hewit? Hewit?" These birds have a beautiful, rolling, whistled song of many notes. They have the irritating habit of opening a song with a note, clear and exquisite, then stopping to swallow a berry or snatch up an insect, delivering another note, making a flight to an adjoining perch, where very probably they forget that they have started a strain, thus leaving the listener in irritated suspense. When one becomes utterly provoked with them, they may remember and finish the strain, or they may take wing, bubbling out in complete spontaneity notes so high and sweet and musical that they wipe out the memory of the former indignity to the feelings. I can think of no words in which to syllabify this song. The orioles have an alarm call, delivered around their nests and young, very clearly uttered and very appropriately, a staccato cry: "Check! Check!" like the blackbird's notes in syllabication, entirely unlike them in delivery.

There are no birds more voluble than orioles, the females having many things to say when they are gathering nest material and while they are busy building. They openly rejoice over every string and hair they find suitable for their purpose. The males are extremely active on wing, and color almost every flight they make with their song as well as their plumage; while the volubility of both parents is inherited by the youngsters, which talk incessantly throughout the day, and keep me awake half of the night, if it happens to strike the parents' fancy to hang their pendent purse a yard from the foot of my bed outside the screen of my sleeping-porch, as a pair of these birds did in the summer of 1916. The youngsters in that nest carried on a conversation all night – sleepy, low chips and peeps – while for several nights after they left the nest, each one of them sang himself to sleep and then sang in his sleep the remainder of the night on near-by limbs. One writer on ornithology has pronounced them "the cry-babies of birdland," but with this I can not agree except in so far as to admit that they keep up a continuous sound; I can discover no complaint or unhappiness about it. It is simply oriole volubility working out in them through the only sound possible to the youngsters in expressing themselves. I am perfectly sure that these notes on the part of the oriole nestlings are not crying, because they are uttered by birds full-fed, in perfect comfort, and during the night, when, they are half asleep.

Some of our writers on bird music find strains, especially in the operatic performances of some of our great European composers, very similar to the strains of the song sparrow, oriole, and a number of our finest songsters. The similarity of these songs to the notes of our birds could be only accidental, since it is highly improbable that any of these composers ever heard our larks and orioles sing.

Associated with the oriole in my mind is the red-winged blackbird, which comes earlier and some seasons nests in large numbers in a strip of swamp directly across the narrow channel of the lake in front of the Cabin. One summer in particular, they crossed the channel and swarmed all over the woods food hunting, scratching over the ground like industrious chickens, pausing with swollen throats and wings half-lifted to deliver their cry beautifully clear in accent and inflection: "Konka-ree." Again, it comes plainly in the call form: "O-kalee!" Their song is nothing more than a sort of whistling-humming: "Gug-lug-a-ree!" These notes are long-drawn, pure, and very sweet.

Meadow larks we have always with us, coming from the cultivated fields adjoining our woods on the south to hunt food in our thickets, vines, and bushes, over the open garden and the meadow behind it. Their tribal call is difficult to render, short, sharp, and unmusical: "Z'stt, z'stt." The notes of no bird of our ornithology are better known than the sweet, lovely song of the lark. In words appropriate to the season and easy to understand, the larks cry: "Spring o' year!" just as distinctly as the whippoorwill pronounces his name. Over the alfalfa fields of Nebraska, I heard meadow larks in tones of sweetness quite equal to our birds add two notes to this strain making it in complete form: "Spring o' year, my de-ar!" a wonderfully lovely song beautifully rendered; while above the Limberlost we had the notes of an English skylark a few years ago, but I fear that he did not survive, as I heard him for only two season.

The night hawk's tribal call is a hiss when disturbed, and his music is usually described as booming, since to produce it the bird flies aloft to a height of eighty feet or more and then drops vertically to earth with extended wings, so that the air whistles through the primaries in a queer, booming sound.

Among the almost songless birds may be classed the cowbird, which sits on the fences with swollen throat, half-lifted wings, tucked tail, and with deep guttural utterances wheezes forth something that sounds like: "Gluck-zee-zee!" these notes being brought forth with such apparent effort that once is as often as the bird delivers them at a time as a rule. Most rules concerning bird music are extremely flexible, since these little creatures, having the freedom of the earth and air, are about as irresponsible as the wind that "bloweth where it listeth," this being a very good description of the manner in which birds sing.

Coming back to the Cabins, we always have the chimney swift, which glues its nest inside the fire place chimneys, seeming to pay not the slightest attention to the smoke of occasional summer fires on chilly evenings. With neither rhyme nor reason and with no particular musical tone nor inflection, they cry above us: "Chip, chip, chip, chippy, chip, chip!" They are beautiful birds of tireless wing and invaluable insecticides.

Another familiar bird of ours which invades the verandas of the Cabin, north, and hunts sweets over the wall-pockets and big jardinières of wild flowers on the broad stone copings, is the ruby-throated hummingbird. These birds come to us surrounded by the humming of their invisible wings so that we know of their presence by their hum and their passage through the air near to or over our heads. With squeaks of delight, they greet masses of blood-red Oswego tea, lavender bergamot, and deep yellow butterfly flower. I have heard hummingbirds, with open bill and distended throat, perching on an ash limb above a widely spreading bed of Oswego tea, sing an amusing murmuring continuous sound that I think undoubtedly they intended for song; but it is even more hopeless of translation than the song of the wren.

Without fail, under the boat-house, under the dock, on the logs of the Cabin, north, and through the woods, every year we have Phoebe birds. The male begins early in the morning, and an unbelievable number of times to the minute for several hours at a stretch, monotonously, insistently, yet in clear sweet tones, he cries: "Phoe-be, Phoe-be!" After screaming for her insistently for four years, the bird at last achieved the triumph of bringing the young lady, who is now taking these cries at my dictation.

A near relative and sweeter singer is the wood pewee, which builds its tiny and exquisite lichen-covered cup on oak and maple branches. He is invaluable as a fly-catcher, being in the same class with his cousin Phoebe, martins, and swallows. His call note is clear and high "Pe-wee!" His song consists of clearly uttered, exquisitely intoned notes, drawn out, accented, and inflected, according to the mood of the singer, usually delicate and of fullest perfection just at the approach of twilight, when most other birds are quiet. At this hour there seldom is bird music, with the exception of the wood and hermit thrushes. The pewee begins on a clear, high note, "pe," drops a fourth, sings "A" and ends a minor third above with "wee." Then he pauses, until you are exasperated with the waiting, and drops in a final note, which is a pure pearl of sound and song, "peer!"

In the orchard of the Cabin, south, and thickets, surrounding the Cabin, north, we have constantly in summer the conversational "Ker-rip?" of the kingbird. Sometimes he asks the question without the hyphen, sometimes he screams: "Quirp!" and again — especially if he is issuing a challenge or threat against any other birds — he cries: "Ker-r-r, Kerr-r-r, Kerr-r-r!" I have the works of at least one writer, who credits this bird with "a soft, pleasing song." I can produce perhaps two dozen pictures of a number of kingbirds about the affairs of home life. He has built his nest and reared his brood, in one instance, not two rods from my back door. I can testify to his beautiful plumage, his valiant disposition, his unusually loving consideration of his mate, and untiring devotion to his young, his implicit trust in me, surpassing that of all other birds, but I never heard one note of this "soft, pleasing song." When he has managed to sing it during my lifetime of acquaintance with him, I can not imagine.

CHAPTER XIII - WHAT BIRDS SAY AND SING

ANOTHER of our friends is the jay bird, a beauty in plumage, friendly in disposition, a good husband and father, but dangerous to the nests and eggs of other birds. His call note is high, clear, and rather antagonistic: "D'jay, d'jay," certainly an obtrusive and self-satisfied note. He asks no favor, courts no bird but his mate. He may utter this cry once or a dozen times. I always get the impression from it that he would not avoid trouble if he met it, and usually he finds it. Perched on a conspicuous branch in early spring, when other birds are singing mating songs, the bluejay sings: "Ge-rul-lup" over and over, making rather an attractive song of it. The bluejay notes that really are pleasing to my ear are those uttered by a number of jays having a party after nesting affairs are over, when they gather in the top branches of a tree and in soft tones tell each other to "fill the kittle, fill the tea-kittle," and there are times, when Father Jay perching near his nest looks at his mate with an expression of extreme devotion, and in whispered, throaty utterances says to her something that sounds to me like "Chinkle-chee-tinkle, tankle, tunkle! Rinkle, rankle runkle! Tee chee, twee?" The jay can imitate perfectly the "Killy, killy" notes of the sparrow hawk or the "Ke-ah" cry of the red-shoulder. For this reason, he can cause undue commotion in the woods. As an interpretation of jaybird character and notes a poem by LeRoy T. Weeks, published in The Century in 1906, is equal to any attempt I ever have seen. I should like to quote the entire poem, but must content myself with a few lines of two verses:
"Saucy imp in white and blue,
What's your title? Tell me true.
Comes the answer, sharp, metallic:
'Smart
Aleck!
Smart
Aleck!'
"In the leaves near by,
Crooning to his nesting mate
Songs beyond me to translate:
'Tear,
Tee,
Twink,
Twee!
Room for twojust you and me!'"

On fences surrounding an old orchard and the horse pasture every season we have the bobolink at the Cabin, north. He is commonly called by his tribal note: "Bob o' link" twice repeated, to which he usually adds: "Spink, spank, spink!" We have few, if any, birds that sing a longer song from the vantage of any fence post or wood stump around our meadow. This veritable music-box pours out his song, the whole of which is an interrupted run, interspersed with his call note and ravishing variations which run high and drop again in a sort of fantasy of irrepressible, spontaneous clearness. Many writers on bird song have been able to follow him through the first two repetitions of his name and a choice assortment of "spink, wink, tink, link," only to be forced to give up when the outpouring reaches flood tide. The description of a bobolink in song which called him an "irrepressible music-box" is the best that I have seen.

There are birds which at times fail us, but I can remember no season during which we have not had goldfinches nesting in the bushes around the edges of the woods, in the woods pasture, and beside the field fences of the Cabin, north. These birds come late, nest but once in a season, and after nesting spend the greater part of their time in country gardens. They pass back and forth from these to the woods, singing on wing, so that they sow the air with warbled notes, impossible to syllabify because they are of such bubbling spontaneity. Our gardens seem to be full of lettuce, vegetable oyster, radish, and flower seeds on which these birds feed, and they flock over and claim possession of the long rows of Mr. Burbank's red and brown sunflowers, the small seeds of which are much more appreciated by them than those of the large variety, which have seeds the size of a grain of corn and are awkward for the small bills of these birds. Flocking over the sunflowers they constantly pass back and forth to each other their tribal call in the form of a question: "See me? See me?" Then they have a shorter, detached cry sometimes uttered in an exclamatory way, sometimes given in answer to the "See me?" call. The nearest anyone has arrived, at this cry rendered in our speech, is: "P'tseet!" I have had considerable experience with these birds and I frequently have heard the male bird give the "See me?" call and the female, brooding or feeding her young the "P'tseet" cry in answer. It appeared to me that these cries were used much as human beings would when a man asks, "Where are you?" and his wife answers, "Here."

There are three sparrows that always home in Wildflower Woods, particularly beside a winding private road leading from the woods across the fields and out to the public highway. In the buckthorn bushes bordering one side of this road, in the grasses creeping to the wheel tracks, in the wild rose bushes, and even under rankly growing flowers, these sparrows are always with us. One is the white throat, with his cry of "Chip, chip," crisply and tersely uttered when about the business of life, changing to nervous and excited tones when a snake or squirrel approaches the nest location. His song, in pure, sweet tones, but of monotonous delivery, is the famous "Old Sam Peabody" so human in utterance that country folk call him the

"Peabody bird." His cousin the chipping sparrow has a call note which is a sharper, more tensely inflected "Chip," and a song of scarcely more than a persistently reiterated note which is the least interesting music of the sparrow family. The field sparrow uses the same call note, very similar to the others, and has a song which he varies in a number of ways. These songs are difficult to put into words, while the musician's ending is almost invariably a roll of piping trills, sweet and melodious. In the length of the road from the woods to the highway, we had seven nests of these birds the season of 1918.

The chewink is a bird which comes to us at every spring migration, industriously scratching the earth among the leaves and roots and making himself extremely familiar all around the Cabin, north, especially in the thickets near the spring. The birds have a very distinctive dress, the male being conspicuous for a black head and coat touched with white on the sleeves and tail, white shirt, and a russet vest never closed in front, merely showing before the folded wings. The female has lovely shades of the same color. Her russet is lighter and where the male is black she is a soft, warm, dust color, a shade as effective as dove color, but difficult to describe. In the business of rearing their young these birds seem to be extremely uneasy about each other. They find almost all of their food on the ground, much of the time scratching among the leaves for it, so that they are the prey of snakes and rodents. The male's call, frequent and distinct, is "Chee-wink?" from which these birds take their name. Sometimes the female answers him with a reproduction of the note in exclamatory form, where his call is interrogative. One pair I worked with more intimately and for a longer time than with any other I have known. The female's answer was always plainly given: "Chee-wee!"

The song of the male bird starts in clear, whistled tones, and is one of those previously referred to as extremely disappointing in its ending. The notes raised to twice eight va., begin on D, rise to A, on to E four or five times repeated. The best translation I ever have seen is that of Thompson Seton, who hears the chewink sing: "Chuck-burr, pill-a-will-a-will-a-will!" Sometimes the musician sings on low shrubbery near his nest, but when he is really giving a concert he selects the top branch of the tallest tree in hearing of his mate and sings the song described, with several variations.

Because of the same coloring, this bird calls to mind the rose-breasted grosbeak, with which I was intimately acquainted in childhood and during my residence in Limberlost Cabin, south. The rose-breasted bird has not appeared to any extent in my new location, nor do I hear his notes save very rarely while in field work. He is conspicuously black and white like the male chewink, but on his white breast there is a splash of purplish-blood-red. His call note is a high "Chink!" which does not very well describe the sound. He makes this cry extremely emphatic when he is anxious about his mate and eggs. His song is lovely, of even tone, continuous, and of almost perfect rendition. These notes are as difficult for an amateur to catch in pitch as the song of any field bird I know. Experts agree as to the attractive character of his song, although they differ in its interpretation, several prominent writers insisting that the bird warbles the notes, a thing I never heard him do in a lifetime of closest intimacy. I know the male bird to be as tender and devoted to the female as is the mate of the brooding dove. It may be for this reason that I find his notes toned and inflected with sentiment; for in much work with set cameras before the nest of this bird it has been my experience that every morning about ten o'clock he enters his nest and patiently broods while his mate takes a bath and finds her breakfast, about which she does not in the least hurry herself, for very frequently she fails to return before twelve and sometimes not until one o'clock.

Always beside the road and through the fields we have "Bob White" calls, and on summer evenings while the female quail are nesting, the males, perched on fence riders, prolong this call into a real musical performance by repeating the first note once and quavering the last, making the song: "Bob, Bob White!" The beauty of this performance depends very largely on the age and experience of the singer; old birds content, full-fed, and having had much experience in life and making music, develop a mellow, pleasing tone.

Two birds of summer, seldom seen but very frequently heard, are the yellow-billed and blackbilled cuckoo. These birds are sneakers, travelling through shrubbery with a serpentine motion equalled only by the brown thrasher. Their nests are crudely constructed, their eggs large and pale blue, the bird's plumage a delicate grey dust color with touches of white on wings and tail, the body long and slender, the head almost hawk-like in shape, with exquisitely cut, curved beak. The tribal call of the yellow-bill begins with two or three preparatory notes and ends with four clear and distinctly enunciated ones. He says: "Ur-r-r-coulp, coulp, oulp, olp!" The black-bill, very similar in shape and color with the exception of his black bill, and almost identical in habits, probably named the species by his cry: "Cowk-coo, cowk-coo, cowk-cu-coo, cowk-cu-coo." This is repeated five or six times. In the scene beside the brook in "The Pastoral Symphony," Beethoven used the song of the nightingale, the call of the quail, and the notes of the cuckoo. If this bird can be said to have a song, it is merely a repetition of its call notes differently accented and inflected.

A bird which reminds me of the cuckoo in the handling of his notes is the whippoorwill, named from his cries singly uttered. These constitute a call note. In trouble, he hisses almost like a hawk. In giving a musical performance, he employs the "Whip-poor-will," cry. The notes are differently accented by different birds, but most of the time in a show performance they manage to quaver the "poor" and one can hear a sort of catch of breath before the falling note, when the quaver is unusually long.

A distinctive note, without which no summer at the Cabin, north, would be perfect, is the clearly intoned, incisive cry of the scarlet tanager. With the Cabin site, which included the song sparrow, there was a tanager thrown in for good measure. The bird does not truly belong to me. He does his courting and food hunting in Wildflower Woods, but he builds his nest every year in a maple tree about six inches on my neighbor's side of the line fence. His tribal call "Chip-bird, chip-bird!" sounds constantly around the garage and through the grounds as near to the Cabin as the woodshed. I never have seen him visit the lake front even once. If I wish to show him off to visitors in all the glory of his bloody coat and black silk wings, I must take them to his location, which he hugs very closely. He is one of the latest birds to arrive, nests but once with me, and although he comes late he immediately takes a cold, which persists throughout the season. The manner of his song suggests the robin, with nothing like the robin's cheerily inflected tones. The tanager is a serene, lazy bird alike in lovemaking, nesting, paternity, and above all in his song. He never voices his utterances with a touch of the joy of the song sparrow or the goldfinch, and as for the emphasis of the cardinal, there is no such vim in his system. I know no combination of syllables that will give an idea of his song, for to reproduce his notes a human being would be compelled to hum and whistle at the same time. Any syllabication that could be strung together would abound in r's and suggest Spanish rather than pure American.

In all my experience afield, no one bird, which I might have expected to meet frequently, has been so scarce with me as the cedar waxwing, which I have met only once while the bird was on a pokeberry debauch. His nest I never have found. I knew him well in my childhood. He was one of the most frequent feeders on our cherry trees, and I once had a living specimen, slightly winged, in my fingers, and had the privilege of minutely examining the soft, exquisitely shaded feathers of his back and breast – not grey, not brown, not olive, not yellow, but the daintiest shades that could be formed from delicate mingling of all of them. His crest was shaped much like the cardinal's but carried mostly in a line horizontal with the beak. There were bars of yellow on his tail and red touches like wax on his secondaries, from which he takes the name of waxwing. His cry is a queer, whistled complaint like a gust of steam escaping from a small pipe, and higher than the last note on a piano. If he has a song, I never have heard it.

A bird with which I am extremely familiar through much experience around his nest, is the red-eyed vireo. His call note: "Preach-er, preach-er!" is constantly used as a nickname for him. His song is so divided and intoned that it lends color to this translation of his tribal call. Wilson Flagg's inimitable interpretation of his song is the best that I have seen. He imagines the little orator standing in his pulpit of leafy green, addressing a feathered audience, at whom he shouts: "You see it! You know it! Do you hear me? Do you believe it?" My enjoyment of this translation of the red-eye's song does not prevent my giving the ideas of another expert in bird music, who sees nothing clerical about the bird and thinks he says: "Tom Kelly, whip Tom Kelly!" How he ever heard or imagined that the bird made a note that could be so translated, is a mystery to me. More pleasing is the version of the third writer, who makes the vireo a gourmand and hears him sing:

"Fat wormsplenty to cat
Gobble 'em updon't delay
Come, deardon't delay
I'm herefly this way."

All these experts do agree upon seems to be that there is a pronounced oratorical effect about the bird's delivery, and that his song is broken into distinct groupings of notes.

The chestnut-sided warbler warbles a strain of bubbling, rolling notes after the manner of his kind, but his call note is a clear "T'see, t'see." To him is attributed the famous rendition of his song: "I wish, I wish, to see Miss Beecher." These words he enunciates as clearly as any killdeer or Bob White I ever heard afield.

Every spring our woods are full of warblers. On a day of warm, drizzling rain interspersed with bright sunshine, in May, 1918, the tall trees, with grape vines and bittersweet climbing in tangled masses through the tops, were used as a landing place for a whole flock of warblers, most of them seeming to be males that had arrived in spring migration during the night or early morning. By slipping into the location and remaining motionless against a tree for a few minutes, I saw countless little painted creatures, gleaming in strong tints of yellow and green, black and grey, blue and rose, while they sang a rolling chorus full of "See-see, zip-zee, wee, wee, tu, tu, 'tswee-e, zillup, zip, zip." Which note belonged to which bird it was out of the question to say in the dense foliage so nearly the delicate yellowish green of many of the birds that it was impossible to distinguish the green and yellow ones until they moved.

I have had several experiences working around the nest of a Maryland yellow-throat, but I can describe his call note no better than to say that it is a sweep of sound, which I can not express in syllables of even the crudest form, but when it comes to a song in tones distinctly human and clearly defined, the yellow-throat sings:"Witchery, witchery" and again: "What a pity," two or three times repeated. Then, like a breath of grace notes, he warbles: "You, you" followed by a clear tide of pure, full song: "I beseech you, I beseech you, I beseech you!" These notes are so clearly uttered and so charmingly intoned that there is no question whatever that the little singer would have his demands granted if he only would go so far as to say what it is that he wants.

Another of our star performers is the catbird, named from his tribal call: "Me-ouw" sometimes cut short and sometimes long-drawn, always of such feline quality that it is easy to see how he gained his common name. As a singer, he is one of our choicest. He sings a mocking conglomeration of high notes of the robin, chat, vireo, several of our best thrush singers, song sparrow, and oriole, while he intersperses this charmingly melodious performance with stray cries of the whippoorwill, killdeer, and quail, and he imitates the whistle of the redbird to perfection. He sings from the bushes, doing his best work by no rule about ten o'clock in the morning. No catbird ever sings twice the same, since he is so purely an imitator that he reproduces not only the sounds of birds around him, but also the crowing of the barnyard cock, the cries of the guinea and peacock, the squeal of the pig, bawl of the calf, the whinny of the colt. I have heard him reproduce even the rattle of wheels on the loose floor of a bridge spanning the Wabash River, while he could imitate the rattle of loose spindles in a cart-wheel to perfection.

I can think of no combination of letters, and I have found none in the writings of any ornithologist, that will reproduce the tribal call of the brown thrasher. It is a weird, wailing, whistled note. Because his song is a medley, it is usually compared with that of the catbird. The thrasher is a larger bird, and his first difference from the catbird lies in the fact that the catbird sings solely to please himself, while in seclusion. The thrasher seems to demand an audience. For exhibiting his best art, he selects the highest perch he can find, where he is sure to attract the attention of every bird and human in sound of his voice. Then, as a rule, he sings out loudly and clearly, although he can drop to a faint whisper of sound when he chooses. His second difference from the catbird lies in the fact that, while he starts in to give a public recital he presently becomes so entranced with his own remarkable performance that he grasps the twig upon which he perches, presses his wings tight to his sides, ruffles the feathers of his breast and back until his wings are obscured, and tucks his tail until a line dropped from the point of his beak straight down would very nearly touch the tail tip. From a widely parted beak he pours out a rolling volume of song that even the most expert collector of birds' records never succeeds in truthfully reproducing. His is a more colorful and spectacular performance than the catbird's, but to me the little grey bird, hanging on an elder over the spring, doing all nature from the goldfinch coasting on waves of summer air above him to the soft gurgle of the running water below, is the more finished performer. To the brown thrasher has been attributed the following advice to farmers:

"Shuck it! Shuck it! Sow it! Sow it;
Plow it! Plow it! Hoe it! Hoe it!"

and by some this has been elaborated to include starting in a hurry, harrowing, seeding, covering, raking in, pushing in, weeding, pulling up, ending with, "Leave it alone!"

The choicest singer that belongs to my personal choir of birds at the Cabin, north, is the wood thrush, a bird which I love to call the "bell bird" on account of the exquisite bell-toned sweetness of his notes. His home is in a spice thicket over and surrounding a pool in the deepest woods behind the ice-house. I am very familiar with this bird, as a number of times I have set up my camera in front of his nest. The tribal call is a wispy whisper. The song, as nearly as it can be expressed, is: "A-e-o-lee." Each note is dropped into the dim green of our woods like a pearl slowly slipping from a thread of pure gold. No bird of field or forest can surpass him, with the exception of the hermit thrush. The hermit is his relative, not quite so highly colored as the wood thrush, even shyer, and more timid, seeking deeper woods and more seclusion for his nest. Many people consider the hermit's song the purest, loveliest bird notes. A free translation of what he sings might be summed up: "Oh fear all! Oh holy! Oh holy! Oh Klr-h-wh! Klr-h!" The wood thrushes sing in slightly faster time, with a touch of passion's more colorful note at nesting time, and I think this also is true of the hermits; but when they sing the latter part of August from four in the afternoon to six in the evening, their notes are pure, cool, high, and passionless so that no other bird's song surpasses them.

One of our earliest arrivals and one that remains with us until late in the fall is an ever-welcome signal of spring with me. I am quite sure that I am wide awake every spring at the sound of the first note of the killdeer over the lake. He always comes calling about half past three or four in the morning, crying in tones that one could imagine were plaintive, if it were not remembered that the bird is coming home and probably as happy to arrive as a human being after a time of exile. I feel bound to claim my location as the home of the killdeer, because he comes to me sometimes in late February, always in March, and stays until late November, and where a bird or human spends nine months out of twelve certainly is the location that could be justly called home for him. This bird has a plaintive tribal call, as it flashes around the lake shore, sweeping low on wing, trying to guard the flashing feet of its young too small to fly. At these times, the old bird cries: "Te-dit! te-dit!" and the youngsters take up this cry in the cunningest baby talk that it has been my experience to hear among any youngsters of birdland.

In commonly accepted interpretation of what the birds say, I once wrote the following for the children of Limberlost Cabin:

BOB WHITE AND PHOEBE BEECHER

Bob White tilled the acres of an Indiana farm,
Phoebe Beecher was his neighbour, full of youthful charm.
As Bob did his farming, Phoebe lingered near.
The birds all helped him woo her, with their notes of cheer.
"Spring o' year! Spring o' year!" larks cried overhead.
"Wet! Wet! Wet!" the gaudy flickers said.
"I'll never finish plowing!" cried the discouraged fellow.

"What a pity! What a pity!" wailed a bird with throat of yellow.
"Yankey! Yankey! Yank! Yank! Yank!" jeered a nuthatch grey.
"Hire old Sam Peabody! Old Sam Peabody!" Bob heard a sparrow say.
"T'check! T'check! T'check!" came the blackbird's pert refrain:
"Phoebe'll never have a man who's scared of a little rain."

"Cheer up! Cheer up! Cheer up, dearie!" the robins sang to Bob;
"Cheer up, dearie! Cheer up, dearie! we'll help you with the job."
"Shuck it! Shuck it! Sow it! Sow it!" advised a bird of brown;
"Plow it! Plow it! Hoe it! Hoe it! Go it! Hoe it down!"

"Bob, Bob White!" the unseen quail whistled from the clover.
"I'm plowing," answered Robert, to the saucy mocking rover.
"Phoebe! Phoebe! Phoebe!" sweet the pewee cried.
"She's coming down the lane," the happy Bob replied.

"Witchery! Witchery! Witchery!" sang a warbler gay.
"She has me worse bewitched," said Bob, "every blessed day."
"Come to me! Come to me!" intoned a woodland thrush.
"Come to me! Come to me!" Bob echoed with a blush.

"I beseech you! I beseech you!" sang a bird of golden throat.
"I beseech you! I beseech you!" Bob caught up the note.
"I love, I love, I love you!" the olive thrush repeated;
"'I love, I love you, Phoebe," the joyful Bob entreated.

"Kiss her! Kiss her! Kiss her!" advised the bobolink.
Bob took his advice and kissed her quick as wink.
Chestnut Warbler warbled: "I wish, I wish to see Miss Beecher"
"Preacher! Preacher!" cried the vireo. "Somebody bring a preacher!"

CHAPTER XIV - BIRD COURTSHIP

THE nesting of birds pre-supposes mating, and of this we of necessity can know very little. Whenever naturalists write largely on the mating of birds, you may be sure they are largely guessing. This function takes place soon after migration; at that time the birds are enjoying the boundless freedom of all outdoors. Save in a very few cases they have no lure to any particular spot and so it is impossible to make accurate and continuous observance of the same pair. They are with us one moment, a mile away a few seconds later, feeding here and there, singing snatches from every inviting perch, making what look like irresponsible dashes of flight wherever fancy leads them. How can one tell which bird he is observing for any length of time or what it is doing?

There are times when we feel assured that certain birds remain mated season after season, and return every year to the same nesting location. As well as I know anything that I can not prove, I know this was the case with a pair of robins which homed with us for several summers at the Cabin, south. My neighbour was sure that for three seasons he had the same pair of orioles. Certain it is that he has had orioles in the same tree, on the same side of the tree, at the same height, and twice on twigs of the same branch. The nests appear exactly the same and the birds pursue the same course in the affairs of life. That they are the same birds he firmly believes, and so do I, but we have no way to prove it.

In the case of last year's birds, there are enough pairs to be mated each year to keep us busy watching and to furnish notes on bird courtship, even if their parents remain paired and make love indifferently a second season, as some suggest. In my experience, this is never the case in a first pairing for a season. Each spring brings its frenzy of pursuit and song in a first nesting. I do think matters take on a more casual aspect in the second and third matings of the same pair. But very little information that can be vouched for is to be had, because with the birds, courting is a thing of flight on the part of the female and of pursuit on the part of the male, and we can not fly – at least, not where birds are courting – so we get only hints and glimpses.

Of a very few cases I can write with assurance. Take the birds which every year live and nest around my home. With some of them their affairs are of broad daylight and for everyone to see and interpret as sanely as possible.

English sparrows are polygamous. One male mates successively with several females. But they are such unspeakable pests they are worthy of mention only to advise their extinction.

Every year we have wrens. The male comes alone and often spends all of a week carrying sticks and twigs by the peck into three different wren houses, singing ecstatically at the entrance to each in turn. Such bubbling, persistent song I never have heard from the throat of any other bird not even the indigo finch. When timed, a wren has sung for an hour in a spring rain. Then one day I suddenly become aware that there are two wrens on the premises busy with nest building. This has gone on for years, but tell how Madame is courted and mated I never can; for with closest watching, I have not been able to catch the slightest glimpse of a love affair. Surely she must be drawn to her male by that outpouring of song, for he never seems to leave the premises.

We have song sparrows with us all winter and song sparrows nest low in the honeysuckle or rose bushes or on the ground, at least three times every summer. Whether they are the same birds we can not be sure, but we rather think they are. We never see but two; their song begins on sunny winter days, grows sweeter and more prolonged with spring; no rivals disturb them after migration and they go about their nesting quietly.

There were never less than a dozen pairs of martins on the windmill at the Cabin, south, but the height was great, and they kept to equal altitude in all the affairs of life, so that nothing can be told of them with certainty. They have homed there for years, but I never have seen a pair mate or had a glimpse of anything that looked like courting. How or where these things happen, no clue can be had from our birds. On wing, at a height of nearly forty feet, it takes sharper eyes than mine to tell which is male and which female.

But the love making of the bluebirds is casual. On the first day that the chirp of a bluebird is heard, several males come around either Cabin and orchard and two or three days later the females arrive. The males court the females and dart at each other by turns, often settling to the ground and fighting stubbornly. One custom of the males in courtship is to pick up a blade of dry grass, carry it into one of the houses prepared for bluebirds, and try to induce the females to enter. They remain around the premises until several pairs have mated and all the houses are filled, and then the others go away.

Whether a low voice is a pleasing thing in a bird, whether signs of constancy, sweet temper, and judicious motherhood can be detected and influence the lover in his choice, who can say? The females perch nearby and seem to await the outcome of the battle for their favor, almost with indifference. When the conqueror of all his rivals presents himself for her favor, the female usually flies away. If she is quite ready to begin housekeeping, she condescends to indicate the fact most casually, and the pair is mated.

Our robins come to us immediately on their arrival from the South. Some of them come in pairs and with the understanding that they are to mate and build within a few days, but not all. Some males come alone, and seem to be seeking a mate for days. Nearly all that can be seen of their courtship is the male chasing away any other male that ventures on the premises. They are very staid and lack the flame and ardor of the orioles or cardinals.

In the fields and woods I frequently see birds mating in the trees, on bushes, and in a very few instances on the ground, but I do not see and can not describe the courtship which precedes these unions. Often I see a male in pursuit of another male, when I am sure he is driving a rival from his preserves. And again, I see a male in pursuit of a female, when I am positive he is making a strenuous effort to win her for a mate.

Of one thing I am sure: birds of very gaudy plumage like the goldfinch, oriole, cardinal, and rose-breasted grosbeak, bobolink, and chewink, have spirits as fiery and flashing as their coats. In courting, they reach a pitch not too strongly described as "frenzy." They pursue the mates they covet with ardor, dash, and courage unknown to birds of somber color like cuckoos, all thrushes, and doves. Their gaudy coloring seems to beget reckless spirits and they go about their courting with an abandon never seen in the shy, slipping creatures of deep wood.

Moreover, they love to display their "coats of many colors." Who ever saw one of these brightly plumaged birds select a deep, lonely, secluded place for a residence? They flaunt themselves in the open, come near houses and the affairs of human life, and exhibit nerve and boldness wholly lacking in the somber, deep forest dwellers. Remember the goldfinch piping on your lettuce heads and sunflowers. The indigo bluebird has built along the public highway and preempted the telephone wires for a choir loft, until as a bird of the wire he rivals the swallow – in confidence in humanity, not in numbers. The fences belong to the lark. From every stake and rider, high post carrying rod-lines, or dead stump, he rolls his song up to Heaven.

The cardinal grosbeak is a bird of the bushes, but nine tenths of the time his bush is beside the road or river. In many instances he locates in orchards and even in grape arbors; and once in my childhood a pair nested on a flat cedar limb not ten feet from our front door. It would seem if there were exclusively "instinctive" action on the part of a bird it would cause this, the brightest of all our songsters, to seek deep wood and seclusion, for every flash of his brilliant body in a conspicuous place is a temptation to the itching fingers of straying and unprincipled gunners.

The bluejay homes in our dooryards and orchards not only in summer, but he or his kind remains with us all winter.

That these brilliant birds love their color and flaunt it where it will oftenest be seen, they prove by living, nesting, and bringing up their families among us and not seeking the seclusion and developing the characters of doves, cuckoos, and thrushes.

I have had more experience with the cardinal than with any other one bird, and once a weakling in a nest held a pair close a first location until they were ready to mate and choose a second. On branches where I had made studies of them while around this nest, I secured two pictures of the male in pursuit of the female. But a second mating of a pair is taken for granted and is carried on with nothing like the ardor of the first. At the time I made this series, the hen bird had a small, calloused spot at the base of the beak, not entirely effaced by time, which she undoubtedly had acquired by striking against a fence wire in precipitate flight during the former courtship.

Doves are quiet, gentle, and almost sickeningly effusive; larks are gay, glad lovers; I have seen a few measures of the stately dance a blue heron executes for the charming of his beloved; and the tender advances of a black vulture are quite the most ludicrous of all my experience in birdland. I hope my sympathy with the birds is as active as that of most field workers, but the humping, shuffling clumsiness of the male vulture's advances and the demure elusiveness of the equally humping, shuffling female, the way she glided from a limb and left him to the surprise of empty space when he confidently expected surrender, were most amusing to me.

Careful study compels me to admit that this is the core of what I know. In comparison with the stacks of notes on building, brooding, and feeding, it does not seem very much. But it tends to confirm my first statement that there is very little anyone can honestly relate concerning the courtship of the birds.

At nesting time, the processes of bird life are so similar to human processes in similar conditions that a warm heart, lack of sound judgment and scientific training cause many people, trying to write on the subject of birds, to sin gravely against the laws of nature, which are distinctly coldblooded. It is so easy to suppose because we do a given thing in a given circumstance that the birds are doing the same thing for the same reason, while there is a strong tendency to humanize them until interest in them is lost. If we look upon the birds as irresponsible beings, needing our protection to survive, our hearts are touched and we strive to repay their benefit to our crops and our joy in their beauty and song with tender care. If we come to feel that they have the same mental processes as we have, there is a sort of inclination to let them shift for themselves, since they are so wise.

The birds are the free wild tenants of field and wood; they are so erratic and so irresponsible in most of their acts, and their range is so wide that for three fourths of their lives little can be learned of them by their closest students and lovers. When they are scattered from east to west, range from the Arctic Circle to Patagonia, and make two migrations yearly, it is impossible to know everything about them with certainty.

CHAPTER XV - NEST BUILDING

AT THE nesting season, for a short time, we may come in close contact with bird life. We may feel that we really understand bird processes; for the language of motherhood during cradle-making is universal. When a location is wanted by a pair, the male often takes the lead, carries sticks and blades of dry grass to one place and another, turning and fussing over the spot as if to indicate to his mate that he has found a first class nesting site.

We see our male robins doing this around the Cabins every summer. Male wrens prepare all the wren boxes on the premises for a nest. Male bluebirds carry nest material to boxes even before the females arrive. If it were true, as some writers assert, that male birds do not assist in nest building, these would be very deceptive and misleading acts on the part of the birds; for by them they surely show the female that they consider a certain location suitable for a nest, and with her consent, will begin building. Our male song sparrows always try to dominate the nesting site; while in the hedge, pairs of these birds are always close together, but it is the female that makes the final choice, and drops the first twig on or coils a hair in the place selected. How far she has been influenced by the male in her selection, no one knows certainly.

On this point my experience differs from some nature writers'. I have photographed hundreds of nests; many of them I have watched in the course of construction; while by the hundred I have carefully picked them to pieces after the birds have finished with them to see exactly what they contain and how they are woven; so I know I am right in the cases with which I am familiar, and to which I confine myself.

The female of tree, bush and some ground builders constructs her nest, by laying a foundation of mud, if she is of the turdidae family, omitting the mud if she is a sparrow, finch or warbler. Then she holds her breast as a model, around which she packs her chosen material as she turns while building the walls; but the male almost always helps carry material. He brings his contributions and drops them on the nest, while the female places and builds them in. On a few occasions, in the absence of the female, I have seen a male enter a half-completed nest and try to place material. He was always picked and chased away immediately on her return, as if he were doing something improper, except in the case of orioles. Their nests are so large, so intricate, that the females seem glad for all the help offered them. The real nest of an oriole, inside the covering purse of plant fiber and string, contains as much fine material, carefully placed, as the average bird structure. The weaving of the hammock necessary to support it is all extra work.

Male wrens are credited with being great workers at nest building by writers of theory who lack experience with the habits of the birds. As this matter never has been rightly explained, it is time someone told the truth about it. We often read articles by writers, who tell about the patient, little male wren carrying sticks and twigs for his nest. There is not a twig in the nest of a wren. I have examined them by the dozens. Their nest is a tiny cup, woven of hair and down, often arched with chicken feathers. The truth is this: almost every box placed for wrens is much too large for their soft, tiny nest; so the male wren spends all the time preceding the coming of his mate, tugging at twigs so large he can not always get them into the box, building a barricade between the entrance and the very small space required for his nest. If half a peck is needed, he carries that many, and if the entrance is large enough to admit sparrows and bluebirds, he partially fills it. So when in answer to his persistent song he wins a mate or his mate returns, he can immediately show every wren box on the premises ready for her work on the nest. In the actual building of the nest, he helps no more than numbers of other male birds. This is the truth of the fallacy for years published and re-published to the effect that the male wren "builds the nest before the female arrives or mates with him," or that he "builds several false nests," to deceive people as to his real location.

The song sparrow carries material to his mate while she is at work – hair and down for lining – making many trips to horse stables, watering troughs, and cow barns for long tail hairs clinging to entrances, fences, and stalls. When I was a child, Mother's carriage pair was white, and I always recognized their hair in birds' nests. I even differentiated Ned's, which was pure white, from Joe's, which was grey, while the brown work horses had black mane and tail, as did an elder sister's pony.

Male bluebirds sit outside their doors with building material and wait until the female comes out in order that they may enter and place it. The robins, which every year build on the logs of the Cabin, in the vines covering it, and on the near-by trees, both work on their nests; the male carries material, the female carries and builds. All of us see this repeatedly; there can be no mistake about it. Male robins are among the birds that frequently enter half-built nests to place material; the females always make an angry dart at them when they catch them doing it, clearly proving that the hen considers it her province to build the nest.

My husband and I once watched the building of a pair of indigo bluebirds. Attracted by the songs from a bird-house in the conservatory, the bluebirds settled in a honeysuckle nearby, where we watched their construction while we worked among the flowers. Both birds carried material, the female building. They used what grass they could find, loose bark of the honeysuckle, and dry leaves beneath it, with the result that their nest was the largest and loosest that I ever saw built by their species.

The martins carry quantities of dead twigs broken from tree tops, and at the Cabin, south, stripped the top of a pear tree bare of green leaves, but at the height of their box on the windmill, I could not tell whether the work was done by males, females, or both. I was puzzled as to what use they made of all of the green leaves they carried, until I climbed to their location to clean sparrow nests from the house, and found the martin nests in construction as green as fresh leaves would make them. All of the birds flew ceaselessly, and I am sure that all of them work.

Among birds of the woods, where male and female are very similar in coloring, such as cuckoos, all thrushes, and catbirds, the only way to tell whether the male and female both work is to see both birds at a nest with building material at the same time. This I have seen in the cases of catbirds, thrushes, and doves, but never cuckoos.

The male catbird keeps near his mate after their union and carries twigs, fine roots, leaves, and grass for their nest.

Both brown thrashers carry coarse sticks for the base and finer material for the lining of their nest, and the female builds in rare instances on the ground, always very low in brush heaps or thorn trees.

One spring, I watched almost the entire construction of the nest of a wood thrush. When I found the location the birds had worked only a short time. Clay had been spread over the branching of two stout limbs on a scrub elm bush and on it was laid a handful of fine roots, thready and fibrous. In collecting abandoned nests, I find clay to be very common, especially among the turdidae family. The following day, the female mounted this heap, pressed down, worked out a hollow in the middle, shaped it to her breast, and interwove loose ends. The male brought her a quantity of fine sticks and twigs which she worked in around the base. Often she left the nest and flew for some particular bit of material she wanted. The third day she daubed the inside with clay, lined it with dry grass blades, and deposited the first egg. The building of this nest required three days' work on the part of both birds, from nine in the morning until three in the afternoon. Substituting different material used by different species, the history of the making of this nest is the history of almost any tree or bush nest one can find.

I can almost hear someone asking: "Why didn't you make a series of studies of the building of that nest?" Impossible! Almost every nest location chosen is in deep shade, among branches and twigs; the building birds move constantly and in a tremor of anxiety. At no other time in their lives are they so shy, secretive, suspicious of man and animal as when building. There is no light for a snap-shot, and too much movement for a time exposure. If a camera could be so hidden that the birds would not discover it, it would be utterly impossible to let in sufficient light to reproduce motion, before the birds have brooded until their eggs have quickened, at which time they will risk much to stay on their nests. When building they are abnormally shy and discreet, and will desert a location, often if they merely feel that it has been discovered. Any attempt to work around a nest in the course of construction would instantly cause the bird to desert and change building sites.

A dove's nest is a ramshackle structure containing only a small amount of material; the male keeps close and helps carry the few small sticks and twigs used. The customary location is about the height of or slightly above the top of the average rail fence. Some nest on fences sheltered by bushes, some in brush heaps lower, some in thorn and wild crab bushes higher. One pair of doves on a fence on the Wabash, having had a low nest destroyed by grazing cattle, at once set about building the highest dove nest I ever have seen, on an elm branch at least thirty feet above ground.

I never have seen cuckoos building, but their nest is such an artless, loosely constructed affair, composed of such a small handful of twigs that it would be no tax if the female carried the material and built alone. Twice in work with perhaps a dozen cuckoo nests, I have come across the abandoned nests of other birds that cuckoos have relined and used. One was the nest of a shitepoke, and the other the nest of a robin. I notice that several writers on natural history describe the cuckoo's nest as "filthy." I have examined them by the dozen in my lifetime, reproduced at least a dozen, and never have I found a soiled nest. I can produce many pictures in proof of this taken even so late as on the day the young leave home.

Only a few days ago I read the amazing statement that some of our cuckoos, like their European relatives and our cowbirds, impose their eggs upon the mercy of other birds. It was especially specified that the nests of robins, catbirds, and others having an egg very similar were chosen. Never have I seen or heard of such a thing as a young cuckoo in the nest of a robin, catbird, or any other bird. I should have to be very thoroughly "shown" before I should believe that these writers are not mistaking the first very large egg of a young robin or catbird in her first nesting for the larger cuckoo egg. Nor have I ever seen a cuckoo give the slightest attention to the nest of any other bird. Cuckoos are lovely in coloring, sedate and calm in temperament, and invaluable in any orchard, as one cuckoo crop was found to contain two hundred and fifty tent caterpillars, which few other birds take on account of the hairs, and two hundred and seventeen fall web-worms. The cuckoo is suited to feeding on caterpillars, as he has a thin, flexible gizzard, especially designed for disposing of hair.

One recent European writer says that the European cuckoo places its eggs in the nests of other birds with its beak, implying that it lays them elsewhere and then carries them to the nests selected. This, I gravely doubt. The birds of my experience have the same habits and characteristics as the European species, but I never see them carrying their young and their eggs through the woods in their beaks. Our cowbirds that have the European cuckoo's habit stand astride the nests of smaller birds and drop their eggs where they want them. The old wood duck does not carry her young, but gives a signal cry, at which they tumble from the nest and scamper to the water. The only egg or bird I ever see in the beak of another bird is being eaten.

Nothing but energetic work on the part of both birds could complete in a reasonable time the deep, compact cup of the goldfinch or the summer yellow-bird, the thick felt-like nest of the black masked warbler, or the pendent purse of the oriole. Picked to pieces, the nests of these small birds prove that they contain half a peck of moss, fiber, fine roots, down, hair, wool, et cetera.

I once watched a pair of orioles building their nest. The first day both birds carried material that looked at the height selected like excelsior and hung it under and over a small elm twig. The second day, the female worked her way into the heart of the hanging mass and began pushing it from her on all sides and lashing it over the twigs above her, while the male constantly carried material to her. The hammock was finished, and on the third day the nest was built inside and an egg deposited, I think. Of course I could not see, but the young arrived allowing that day as the beginning of incubation.

The rose-breasted grosbeak breaks off and carries most of the dead dry curlers of wild grape, of which her artless nest is constructed. The male frequently enters a nest and tries to help build. Usually he is picked when he does it, but then he is a hen-pecked husband anyway.

The cardinal is quite willing to help build his nest, but his disposition is so fiery and he becomes so excited that he accomplishes very little actual work, often betraying a location and driving his exasperated mate to begin work anew in a more secluded spot.

I have one wood-thrush nest study, in which the entire nest is made from the fine, red roots of wild raspberries and nettles. These were dug fresh, woven into the nest while wet, and lined with very fine roots of the same. When dry, the complete structure was a bright red brown, nearly as hard as spun glass, and with the full clutch of blue eggs made one of the loveliest nests I have ever pictured.

Enlargement of several kingfisher negatives, where the male and female appear on one plate, proves that the beak of the male was more scarred than that of the female, from working out their tunnel in the back wall of an abandoned gravel pit. There can be no question of the male's having performed the greater share of the work on their home. The wall opening of the tunnel to the nest was three feet from the top of the quarry, six inches wide, four high, and five feet long. When the excavation reached this length, it turned sharply to the right, and a room about the size of a boy's flat-crowned straw hat had been made. All the stones, gravel, and clay in the hard wall that had been loosened had been pushed the length of the tunnel and formed a heap as big as a bushel basket eight feet below, on the edge of a frog pond. Some believe that all this earth and stone is carried out in the beaks of the birds, but this seems incredible; while the appearance of the heap suggested that it had been shoved out. The bottom of the tunnel was concave the size of the birds' breasts, with a groove at each side worn by the feet.

The sitting room was large enough for the male to share it at night. The nest was a rim of fish bones, crayfish shells, grasshopper bones, and berry seeds that the brooding bird had regurgitated in a wall around her. After the young were a few days old, I dug into the tunnel, where it entered the nest, cutting out a piece of surface sod, and arranged a board to support it. In this way, I had access to the nest while the old birds were fishing. I frequently removed and photographed the young. At the same time, I began training the old birds to become accustomed to a camera, focused on their location from the top of a tall ladder, set up in the frog pond below the nest. During the winter, the rains ran into the opening I had made, causing the tunnel to cave in. On their return in the spring, the same pair of birds dug another tunnel and nest not two feet north of and on a line with the first. The face of the wall from a distance looked like that of a frowning giant, having deeply set eyes. I always have felt rather conscience stricken over imposing this second task of tunneling on these birds. They surely were experts, taking turns at the work and completing the heavy task in ten days.

I never have seen larks or bobolinks construct their nests, so I do not know whether these males work. I should think probably not. There is little they could do. Their nest is built by the female sitting down and turning around until she has a small hollow worked out in the earth, which she lines with bits of dead leaves and grass, picked up near her, and slightly arched with growing things pulled together above her; at times the nest is wide open. Bobolinks love to build in clover fields, larks in grasses.

The quail I have seen build, and she does it in this way and alone; although the male remains near her and is very faithful in the care of an emerged brood. The hen broods twenty-four days, during which time rankly growing fence corner grasses envelop her, each day hiding her more completely.

Chats, flycatchers, and vireos build in trees such elaborate nests that it is probable that the male does a large share of carrying material at least.

The daintiest nest I ever have seen is that of a hummingbird in my possession. It is set on a limb scarcely larger than a lead pencil, a shallow cup that a silver dollar will cover, the outside walls covered with bits of lichen bound on with cobwebs, the interior lined with chestnut burr down, as fine as silk velvet.

Next to this comes a gnatcatcher nest, slightly larger, higher in side walls, with moss lining, and the outside very similar.

The nest of a wood pewee is larger in circumference, lower in side wall, similar in lichen covering with cobweb fastenings. All these nests appear like small knots on the limbs where they are placed. All of them are wonderful examples of the highest art in nest building and perfect examples of protective coloration.

The nests of warblers are tiny, hair-lined cups, while goldfinches and indigo birds build deep cups of many different fine materials in crotches or where small twigs branch. The yellow-breasted chat builds in the same manner using slightly coarser materials. She is credited with introducing an occasional cast snake skin, as do the wood thrush and crested fly-catcher.

No birds build lovelier nests than the vireo family, which lash a perfectly round cup by its rim at the intersection of small twigs, and then deliberately decorate its exterior with spider-webs in clots, and the finest outside birch peelings like silk tissue.

So lavish are these birds in the use of cobweb festoons that the possibility is suggested that they are intended to trap tiny flies and insects.

Orchard orioles use lengths of grass for their pendent purse; Baltimores, plant fiber and string. As birds increase in size, they use heavier material up to the big, coarse structures of hawks, herons, or eagles.

Among the "lilies" of the bird field that neither "toil" nor "spin" are the males of marsh and water birds that are ground builders, such as the coot, grebe, rail, and duck. Take the rail for an example. Undoubtedly the choice of a location depends upon the fact that a certain spot slightly above water offers all the material required for a nest. The female snips the green blades of this year's grass from as large a place as she wishes for her nest. Then she steps in among the crisp, dead grasses of last year, breaks them off with her feet, and sitting down turns around repeatedly, at the same time gathering all dry grass blades with her beak and working them into a slight rim around her breast. Then she catches this year's green, growing blades outside her location above her head, and literally ties them into knots. With material needed in reach, and granted that the female is the architect, really there is nothing for the male to do. The case is similar with the other water birds mentioned.

The experience of my whole life afield, all my convictions based on hints and glimpses, and all the proof that can be adduced from my negative closet show that the tie between birds is strong enough that the male helps build the nest, frequently carries morsels of food to the brooding mother, especially in the first days after the emergence of the young, when they must be fed and are too tender to be left uncovered; he remains close to his family at all times, holding himself ready to risk his life for his nest, in case of an attack of any kind. The nest is the objective point around which both old birds hover, and they even follow the young afield and feed them until they look as large as their parents. I have had much experience with the devotion of male birds to their nests, for every time I set up a camera before a bird home, I have the fears of the male to allay before there is any hope that the female will enter her nest and brood before my lens. Several times I have photographed a male bird standing guard on the edge of a nest containing eggs, and once as he entered a nest to brood while his mate went to bathe and drink.

After lending what assistance they can in nest building, most males select two locations nearby, and when not feeding and exercising they sing to their brooding mates. One indigo bluebird, whose mate brooded in a clump of horse-weeds along the levee between the Wabash and the outlet of the Limberlost, sang so persistently from one stretch of telephone wire nearest his nest that for all of one season, I could take friends from cities there and tell them with all assurance that they would see and hear him.

It was the persistent singing, from one branch, of a male wood thrush that led me to his location and a series of the affairs of his life. The rose-breasted grosbeak sings morning and evening near his mate, and when he relieves her while she goes for her morning bath and food, he resignedly enters the nest and settles himself to brood until noon, which is what I meant by calling him a hen-pecked husband. Most male grosbeaks can be found brooding every morning between nine and twelve. I have recorded this repeatedly.

If a dove does not brood on his eggs, he spends hours brooding beside his mate, as near her as he can crowd. Bobolinks keep close to their mates, and their bubbling song and chatter are unending. What a treat it would be, if we could have what they are saying translated for our understanding!

The material birds use in building, manifestly must be what their locations afford. As a rule, there is nothing they can use except twigs, leaves, grass, plant fiber, roots, bark, mud, lichens, moss, snake skins, thistle and milkweed down, and cobwebs in the woods; and these same things combined with wool, string, rags, papers, horse-hair, and feathers in the fields. Because they must use these things or build no nest, they use them. But their use of them does not prove that if they could go into a store and buy a yard of yellow and red calico and tear it into strips for nest material, they would not be delighted to do so; for by every act of their lives the birds prove that they appreciate color.

I am aware of the fact that in all probability that statement will be challenged; but I am ready for the challenge. If birds do not appreciate the gaudy colors on their backs and love to flaunt in the open showing themselves before men, how does it happen that cardinals, orioles, bluejays, bluebirds, goldfinches, rose-breasted grosbeaks, tanagers, and almost without exception our brightest birds live in the open and are constantly seen; while thrushes, cuckoos, doves, and birds of somber color seek the deep wood and slip around as if in hiding?

If there were any such thing as "instinct" in this matter, these inconspicuous birds, perfect examples of protective coloration, would be the ones to live by roadside and stream, where their color would save their lives; and the bright birds would hide in deep wood and slip around unnoticed, for every flash of their gay color in a public place is a challenge to unprincipled gunners. But who ever heard of a cardinal "slipping" in any location? He is generally in the most conspicuous place, displaying himself before men. It seems as if the bobolink dances on the fences, and literally rubs himself into one's attention. Every brilliant bird is out where he will show, and if one does not see him, he manages to make sufficient disturbance or call one's attention with his song. Did you ever see a peacock after his tail had been plucked? I have known them to be so ashamed, so humbled over their loss that they hide until they almost starve to death before they will show themselves in the open to take food. Does anyone, who has ever seen a peacock strut, doubt that the bird is proud of his tail or that he suffers near to death on losing it? Birds of the open evolved in the open. Their native food and nest locations are there. Bright light produced the gay plumage on birds, just as it produced the strongest yellows, reds, and blues on flower faces of the open swamps and fields, and kept the fragile, pale ones in deep shade.

Of the hundreds of nests of which I have made studies, and picked to pieces after the birds have finished with them, every nest proves that birds, even the shy, slipping, deep wood creatures, avail themselves of bright material wherever possible. I have seen summer yellow-birds use so much milkweed down that their nests fell prey to crows and hawks on account of being so conspicuous. After building a pendent cup, firmly timbered and lashed to a branching limb, red-eyed vireos festoon cobwebs over the front of it; and before a set camera, one bird added fresh cobwebs to a nest from which one of her young had already taken wing. The cobweb was simply draped over the front of the nest, and not used to bind on outer covering or lash a nest to a limb, as cobwebs are used by flycatchers and hummingbirds. This nest also had curious tiny seed pods stuck over the front of it, for purely ornamental purposes.

A small collection of the nests of vireos was sent me from Cuttingsville, Vermont, in 1918. The home of the warbling vireo was gay with the delicate, white tissue of the outer bark of birch trees and cobwebs draped over the pale fawn color of the primary decorations, among which were several bits of newspaper. On one of these, the words, "clock for mantle" could be read distinctly. The house of the red-eye was much the same only whiter; while the yellow-throat used none of the colored bark, almost completely covering the dark nest material with white paper, white birch fringes, and snowy cobweb. All of these nests would have been almost impossible to distinguish from their surroundings, had it not been for the lavish use of conspicuous material.

Shrikes use so many chicken feathers around their nest rims that they sometimes infest their young with lice, and one shrike nest I reproduced had a roll of grey wool at the top.

One kingbird nest was conspicuous on account of the use of large tufts of black and white wool and cotton cord strung around but serving no purpose. Wood thrushes and chats use cast snake skins, which are showier than most nest material. These skins are no component part of the nest, but festooned over the outside as an ornament; and so far as I can learn, are used only by these birds and crested flycatchers which build in hollow trees. It has been suggested that these birds use the snake skin as a means of protection to their nests, but this grants the birds power to plan and think. However, there is some reason why only these three birds use the skins, which I frequently find afield but never in the nests of other birds. Very peculiar things, which evidently have been carried from houses some distance away, can be found in quite secluded nests.

Many women can testify to having had orioles snatch bits of bright ribbon and yarn for weaving into nests from work baskets left on verandas. I went to my front veranda one spring to wipe a soiled place from a window. Someone called me inside, so I laid my cloth on the railing, and went to see what was wanted. On my return the cloth had vanished; after a thorough search, I discovered a pair of robins gleefully tugging at it on the branch of a big elm tree nearby. It served as a part of the foundation of their nest. Luckily, they found it so early in their work that the other material almost covered it; the nest was not so conspicuous as I feared it would be. One summer, a pair of robins that had previously built two nests of material gathered in the orchard, near the Cabin, south, had just laid the foundations of a third nest in a plum tree beside my bedroom window, when they discovered a bundle of long, white, newspaper trimmings that had been used for packing. Instantly those birds abandoned what would have been considered "instinctive" or natural material, and with such chatter and excitement as I never before heard from brooding birds, both of them attacked the paper. They had to fly much farther to secure it than the material they had been using, while it was in long strips, troublesome to carry and place. Tags two feet long streamed from the birds as they flew and the completed nest on all sides. This paper and mud to hold it were the only materials used after its discovery. The nest was as large as a half-peek measure and snow white. It was so conspicuous that it required constant watching by all of us to protect it from sparrows, jays, hawks, owls, and cats attracted by it. All winter it stood, while rains and winds did their worst. The following March that nest remained the most prominent feature of the backyard.

Anyone who desires can prove for himself that the birds will leave such material as they can glean from nature, and build a nest rivaling the rainbow, by cutting bright rags and string and scattering them over the ground and bushes, where nest material is being gathered. Understand, I am not advising people to do this systematically, for every particle of bright material used in the construction of a nest advertises it to all of its natural enemies. I am only pointing out how my statement can be proved if doubted.

I have gone further and placed gaudy rags and yarn beside twine and plain colors. The birds see the plain material, because they use it, after the last shred of bright stuff is gone. Here is another problem for believers in instinct only. If birds build by instinct, why do they persist in using bright stuff, foreign to natural selection, that will inevitably end in the destruction of their nests?

Not only do birds build of surprising material when they have the opportunity, but they build in queer places, without question foolishly chosen. If "instinct" guides their selection then it is often sadly at fault. I find nests on the ground where it is inevitable that they will be trampled by herds of cattle, overturned with the plow, torn by hay rakes or reapers. Often they are on bridges and fences, where they are picked to pieces by the first passing boy. They are in bushes in plain sight of roads and pathways, when if placed a few yards farther back, they would be effectually concealed. Birds build in clearings, where the trees are falling fast, and it would seem that any degree of foresight would teach them that their tree would go next. Once, in a clearing, a pair of doves built a nest in a brush heap and the hen deposited her eggs, between the time the cuttings were stacked and the workers were ready to apply the torch. Luckily, that nest was on our land and I could order the workers to leave the heap and give it all possible protection, or that nest would have been burned three days after it was built. A pair of wrens built in a sprinkling can that was hung in a tree to drain, and a pair of robins on the cross beam of a hay rake left standing in an open field. I previously described the nest built on a freight car. Last summer, I was called to the backyard of a neighbour to take a picture of a nest of a wren, built in the hip pocket of a pair of trousers hung on the line. The garment was left until the wrens had finished with it.

On our dock at the Cabin, north, during the summer of 1918, I ran my hand into a bait can left standing a few hours – one of the small tin cans four and one half inches high and three inches in diameter – and found it contained the nest of a bird. I thought it had been placed there by some member of my family for a joke. I thought possibly my driver had found it and put it where he thought I should be sure to notice it; but most of all, I thought it looked so dainty, so fresh, so fitted to its place that, although I knew the can was half full of fresh grub and living angle worms, I stood it back on the seat where I found it. Inquiry elicited the fact that no member of my family knew anything about it. The next day, the cook, fishing from the dock, reported that she saw one of the prettiest little yellow birds she ever had seen enter the can. I went to see, flushed a prothonotary warbler, and found an egg. The next day she failed to deposit an egg; the following three consecutive days she filled out the clutch, then brooded, and reared her young, which all left the dock safely, All the time, the bait can stood on a seat running along one side of the dock. Many birds bring off broods from the most unwisely chosen locations. Every year I see nests destroyed in large numbers through the injudicious site selected by the builders.

On the other hand, nests can be found adroitly placed in such secure positions that the only way one ever finds them is by stumbling over them. I have known many birds that brought off full broods in trampled pastures, by locating under the base leaves of big pasture thistles, under logs, gnarled roots, and stones. While some birds build in the open, others hide in deep wood and conceal nests with a foresight which seems uncanny. It is certain that birds learn by experience. One is left to wonder in summing up if there are not wise and foolish birds, and if these nests in ill-chosen places are not the first attempts of last year's birds that will learn by experience.

Bird architecture proves experience and even wisdom on the part of some builders. I have in my possession the nest of an oriole, built like every other nest of its kind save that under the limb to which it is fastened there is framed a window large enough to admit the bird's head for light and air, and if necessary it could be used for egress. The nest was in a cottonwood, and the limbs were large and heavy for oriole use. The limb to which the nest was attached formed the upper sash, the lower was a loop of cotton cord, firm and strong. Over this loop, the nest material was passed and drawn down into the body of the nest so closely that it was more deftly finished than at the top. Evidently the builder had decided on having this window, for a first attempt too high for use had been begun and abandoned for this one at just the right height.

It was impossible for this oriole to build this window without knowing for what purpose she intended using it; in fact, it required thought to plan and construct it. She had to remember the confinement and inconvenience of former nests, and determine that in the future she would obviate these difficulties. So remembering the past and providing for the future, in this nest she built a window. She did not build it "instinctively" or the trees would be full of oriole nests with windows. She was in advance of her time, and if her progeny follow her example, coming generations may see all orioles building windows. This certainly would be an improvement, for as these nests are built at present the brooding bird is dropped into a deep purse, with no ventilation except at the top, and no way to see a threatening danger in time to avoid it. How this bird must have enjoyed sitting with her head out of the window while she brooded, thus having light and air and seeing any danger to be avoided! Moreover, if she did make this window large enough to admit the passing of her body, as it appears to be, it would furnish her a chance to escape in case she was attacked by a night hawk or screech owl at the top of her nest. In the construction of the hammock for this nest the bird carried a piece of cotton cord from the nest, passed it around a limb, tied it into slip knots and then incorporated the loose end in the body of the nest. It can also be proven that the window idea is beginning to exist among birds, for after six years of search among the trees around the Cabins I found evidence that another oriole made the same attempt, but not very successfully as her window was planned in the same way but was too small for use. Disappointed in this the bird then greatly shortened the length of the hammock in which her nest swung, so that she could brood with her head free. There is no room for argument about these nests; their structure proves what I record of them.

A careful study of building and brooding birds, at least in the intimate relations required in making photographic studies of them, will convince most people that different birds of the same species have different degrees of mentality and different characteristics. Some are friendly and confiding, and soon learn to trust one. Some are so nervous and wild it takes patient work to win their confidence, and some can not be won at all. Some build in well-chosen places and make their work secure, and some select their locations so unwisely they see their nest destroyed before it is complete; so it goes, very like humanity after all.

CHAPTER XVI - HOW THE BIRDS KNOW

THOSE creatures that crept from prehistoric slime, later developing feathers, are older than man. These early birds had heavy jaws, teeth set in sockets, claw-like fingers on the first wing joint, and long, jointed tails having feathers running down each side. Coming down through the ages since that time, our birds of to-day have lost their teeth through lack of necessity for them; have developed such power of flight that the wing claws have become useless and vanished until they are now represented by only a tiny, blunt tip at the first joint; the encumbering jointed tail has contracted in almost every species to an inch or less of tiny, closely set vertebrae, while miraculous power of flight has developed.

Birds that remained on the water evolved flat, boat breasts for swimming, grew webbing between their toes to make them efficient paddles, and shovel-like bills for scooping up wet, wormy food. In sharp contrast with them, the birds of the shore line grew narrow, slender bodies, extremely long legs developed from constant wading, no webbing between the toes, remarkably long pointed beaks, designed for probing for food among the stalks of growing rushes and watery vegetation – such birds as storks, cranes, and herons.

Birds that sought the mountains and remote places grew wide tireless wings, eyes of magic from constantly sighting food at long distances, and stout, sharply hooked beaks for tearing it up. Those that homed in caves and hollow trees in their dark confinement developed enormous eyes, surrounded by feather reflectors, softly feathered short wings, stout feet for seizing prey, and thick necks with wide gullets for swallowing what they captured whole.

Then a large body of small birds that took to the open country evolved, some the long sharp beaks of fruit-eaters; some the hard short beaks of seed-eaters; all bright eyes, great agility on wing; in most families, exquisite song.

As our planet shook itself together, settled, and took up the business of following an orbit, it began growing fruit and vegetables, which developed seed, while revolution and rotation resulted in changing climatic conditions until the birds acquired the habit of following the seasons from north to south in search of the food suitable to each species.

It would be foolish to claim that our birds of to-day have learned nothing during all these ages of constant change. Man has evolved from his cave or his garden, to his present state of form, feature, and accomplishment. Equal to, if not antedating him, the birds have kept pace with him in evolution, the difference being that man develops after the manner of human beings, while birds develop after the manner of their kind. Man is endowed with a reasoning, thinking brain, which grows more capable by being used through the ages. The birds are equally well endowed after a different manner. It is not theirs to reason and think as man does, yet if left in wholly natural conditions the birds know more than man. Man becomes lost in a trackless waste; the birds know the way across great deserts or a thousand miles of water. Man has often starved in the open; the birds know what food they may take with safety. Man learns through his own experience and by heeding the experience of his ancestors. The birds learn a different lesson which is their birthright. How much they know, we can only guess by what they do. We can know how far they fly through a close study of migration. We learn how far they can see when we watch a hawk or eagle drop unerringly from the clouds and snatch up a snake from earth.

We know of their devotion to each other, because we constantly see birds risking their lives in defense of a mate or nestling. We know that they can communicate with each other, because we constantly hear them call and answer, see numbers of them aroused by the curiosity of one, see a whole flock take wing at the warning of one, see them fight over food, see them exhibit the very human attributes of love, anger, greed, suspicion, curiosity, pride, et cetera.

We know that they have a spine, on the top of which sits a skull, enclosing a brain, also provided with fine eyes and a beak for taking food and to be used in self-defense. To what extent a bird uses its brain, it is impossible for a human being to state. Whether we believe that birds act solely upon "instinct" or exercise the brain, as they do the eyes, feet, wings, and the remainder of their anatomy, we are all forced to concede one thing: no matter by what name we call it, the birds know. Exactly how much they know, and exactly how they know it, we can only surmise. This thing is sure: as the ages go by, they are gradually improving, even as man progresses. Since the birds' ancestors crawled from the water and took up life upon the land, they have fallen into divisions, based upon the locations in which they remained. These divisions have now become so distinct that the form and habit of each bird are suited to life upon the water, on shore, or mountain, or in the cave, hollow tree, or field. They have learned to migrate, to build their nests, and what to feed their young, each after its kind. They are not the same creatures that crept from the original slime of things to begin life that had flight as the eventual means of transportation. They have moved forward in a slow, steady progression, directed by a form of knowledge the source of which we can not divine, since they are birds and we are human beings.

We feel that the birds are closer kin, of greater interest, more nearly paralleling our life processes than are forms of life lower than they. Yet to all lower life, no matter how lowly, we must grant the power to know how to live after the habits and characteristics of its kind. The life processes of a bee or ant are more complicated than those of a bird, yet these tiny creatures, which would make the average bird but a small mouthful, have the same knowledge of how to live their lives.

There seems to be no room for comparison between an oriole, exquisite in color, tireless of wing, of beautiful song, weaving her complicated hammock of plant fiber in which to swing the nest for her eggs and young, and a squashy, big caterpillar on a hickory twig beside her. It is difficult to discover eyes, brain, or much power of locomotion in the worm, yet if that caterpillar is taken from its hickory twig and carried a long distance, in case it is a regalis, it will travel in a straight line to the nearest hickory tree, which it will climb, feed through a series of moults to maturity, descend to earth, burrow to a depth of six inches, prepare its winter residence, cast its skin, and take on the form of the moth, which emerges in the spring. At the proper time, the moth will appear, take wing, mate, find a hickory tree, and deposit her eggs on the undersides of the leaves, which are best suited for food for the tiny caterpillars when they emerge. Then the moth will nestle down in the grasses and pass out, never having taken food herself. The tiny caterpillars leave their shells knowing upon what leaves to feed, how to conduct themselves during a series of moults and how to take their part in all the processes of their lives, even more unerringly than the birds, for I have frequently seen birds make mistakes. I never saw a moth or caterpillar make a mistake, unless it had been subject to some outside interference. Whether the caterpillar of to-day enters a different pupa case or spins a better cocoon than those of the first century, I do not know; but I think they do, since creatures that have performed the same operations since their evolution to the cocoon stage should attain great facility. By several forms of conclusive evidence, I hope to prove that the birds are progressing.

The aged Simeon Pease Cheney, for fifty years a professional musician, after a lifetime of bird friendship and study, at the age of sixty-seven, began recording bird songs for a book. Unfortunately, he was unable to complete it. Shortly before his crossing, he used the expression: "The birds improve." He had reference to the development of their voices from the first guttural squeaks, screams, and cries of prehistoric forms to the exquisitely modulated notes of to-day, which should go on increasing in number through notes learned from each other and in timbre with the constant use of the vocal chords. I am satisfied that our birds of to-day sing truer to form, more surely modulated notes than the birds of the ancients; while I can not conceive the delicacy, the molten sweetness that ages to come will hear. There is no way to estimate how long the birds have been singing; when we recall that the oldest bit of translation existing in the world is the lament that "the good old times are gone forever," this seems a very old world indeed.

The birds have been building longer, in all probability, than they have been singing. Here a change can be better noted. In my personal experience, it appeals to me that the hummingbirds and gnatcatchers build more nearly perfect nests. I know that the vireos of my childhood went to no such extent in decoration as that family goes to-day. Vireo nests were compact, dainty, and lovely, but I never saw them decorated with unique seed-pods, snow-white festoons of cobweb and birch tissue, and newspaper, as the nests reproduced in this book.

The oriole nest with a window is an arresting thing. This nest could not have been built "instinctively" since the bird possessed no inborn instinct to guide her in its construction. It could not have been built through a subconscious impression from her ancestors, since they did no such building. It is going beyond any mentality I have ever attributed to a bird in natural history work, but this nest proves a number of separate mental conceptions on the part of the bird. She had to realize the confinement of her usual structure, which gave her no means of escape in case of attack from above. She had to resent her shut-in condition while brooding, and decide that she would try to remedy it. The nest proves her first trial a failure. She outlined a window and began weaving around it; then realized that it was too high for her to brood and use it at the same time. So she abandoned her first effort and designed and completed her window where she could sit on her eggs, and at the same time, have light, air, and a view from her location. Also, the window was large enough to afford her means of escape in case a squirrel or screech owl attacked her from above. This nest was also stayed at one side so it would hold firmly in a gale. Notice the lashing of cord that runs from the nest to the branch which holds it at this twig, where it is plainly tied in two slip knots, then carried back into the body of the nest. The heavier stay wound several times around the top limb outlines the window and is then carried below and looped around the limb, brought back, and woven into the nest. The entire structure gives evidence of extraordinary skill in construction, resulting from what we should call "original thought and plan" in the case of a human, since the bird to my knowledge had no precedent. If orioles the world over have been building with windows, and tyingslip knots scientists and natural historians have forgotten to mention it.

I reproduced two views of this nest in a book of mine, "Friends in Feathers," published in 1917. Ever since, I have hunted for oriole nests, hoping to find other birds in rebellion against accepted form, but with no success until the spring of 1919, while I was at work on this book, one of my field men brought me the nest here reproduced. This bird had attempted a window and failed. She made it too small and too high. Lacking the ingenuity and brain power of the other bird, yet having the window idea in her head, she compromised by shortening the hammock, in which she swung her nest, until raised by the diameter of her eggs, she could brood and look from the top of the nest. Truly, the old bird lover was right when he said in passing: "The birds improve."

Quite as remarkable as the oriole nests with windows is a double vireo nest, found and photographed by Professor Lynds Jones, ornithologist of Oberlin College, reproduced in Dawson's "Birds of Ohio." Professor Jones found this nest in Iowa, and graciously permits me to reproduce it here. The twin nests would not be so remarkable – female birds often locate in colonies or near each other – had the nests been the work of two females; but Professor Jones asserts that the double structure was built by one pair, that the female divided her eggs between them in laying, while both male and female were brooding when he found the nest. I can not attribute the work on this structure either to "instinct" or "subconscious mind." It appeals to me as plain knowledge. The birds surely knew that they were building two nests and why they built them. The hen knew she was laying in two nests and the male bird that he was brooding when he occupied one of them. Nothing more remarkable than this ever has occurred among the birds to my knowledge. My oriole was the originator of the comfort of a window for the basement of labour for her sex, but this vireo in building two nests and halving the labour itself was ahead of her. These signs of the times surely indicate progress in birdland. If our feathered sisters are demanding improved homes and equal sharing of the labour of rearing families, this may be a hint to women who need convenient homes and help in family cares. Let the men "improve" or beware!

If I have less to say than might be expected on the subject of what the birds know, consider a moment and you will realize that there is very little anyone can advisedly relate on any phase of bird life outside of nesting time. It must be remembered that for four or five months the birds, which we call ours, are hundreds of miles away; so no one can say certainly where they are or what they are doing. Again, while they are with us, except for the short space of time when they are bound to their nests by the brooding fever, they are shy, wild citizens of all outdoors. No other living creatures have the freedom of the birds, accorded them by their power of swift flight. They spend their lives snatching bits of food here and there, swaying on every inviting twig, playing tag with a friend, in hot pursuit of an enemy, trailing broken notes from every available choir-loft, with us one minute and a mile distant the next. Who can write of them with absolute certainty? Also, in many cases, the sexes are so alike they can not be told apart in freedom without glasses, and when they differ, all males and all females of the same species resemble each other so closely that it is a dubious guess, with the exception of nesting time, as to how long one can observe the same bird.

One thing that they know is when to migrate and when to return to us, for there is no question but certain birds do return season after season not only to the same state and county, but to the same vine on the veranda and the same knot-hole under the eaves. What determines the precise minute of their starting to come to us or to leave us, or how they follow their trackless path high in air across seas and continents mostly under cover of darkness, we do not know. The birds must know, since barring disaster, they arrive, prompt to the day and almost to the hour.

I often read of "the birds that remain with us in the winter." The birds that remain with me are very few, confined almost entirely to owls, which if undisturbed will spend a lifetime in one hollow tree. I have other birds in winter, but I have no way of proving that they are the same birds which have been with me during the summer. Instead, I think that it is very probable that they are birds which have spent the summer farther north and now make their migration to us, while ours of the same species have gone farther south. This marvellous knowledge, which guides them and enables them to perform miracles, almost passes the comprehension of man. Birds of many species have such unerring knowledge of the workings of nature that they migrate when it is necessary and remain where they are when it is not. For example: during the bitter winter of 191718 when extreme cold began in November and lasted in such prolonged form that we experienced killing frosts in June, there was not a robin in the swamps and gullies or deep woods surrounding Limberlost Cabin, north. In the unusually mild winter of 191819 these birds never left us. In flocks of half a dozen, at any time during the winter, they could be found in the spice thicket back of the garage or in the sheltered ravines, and their appearance indicates that they are living fatly upon dried berries, frozen fruits and vegetables, and food which they pick up in chicken-parks and around the farmers' back doors.

Our bluebirds, cardinals, robins, doves, king-fishers, and other hardy ones in our extremely cold winters go farther south, frequently stopping in Kentucky and Tennessee. Often some of the cardinals remain all winter or others come from the north. One of our ministers to Mexico told me that there are cardinal grosbeaks exactly like ours in Old Mexico all the year, but there are three times as many there during our winter. Our wrens, thrushes, bobolinks, and blackbirds proceed to the coast. Our orioles go to Panama, and hummingbirds to Brazil; our kingbirds and some bobolinks go as far south as the West Indies and Bolivia; and most of our warblers stop in Central America; but some of our thrushes go on to Peru; the golden plover ranges to Patagonia, and the knot to Cape Horn. Exactly where the swallows go is their secret. It is supposed to be some island east or west of South America or to some inland cave. So far, no one has learned where they winter.

The impulse to migrate is so ingrained in the birds with their evolution through the ages that it is a matter of life and death with them. When migration time comes in the fall, the birds of a family begin flying around, uttering their tribal call until large flocks of them gather. Then with one accord, for the most part under cover of darkness, they take wing and fly until they reach their southern home. In some species, the males leave first. Our ruby-throated hummingbird is accused of deserting his nest while his young are quite small, leaving the female to finish feeding them and remain with them until they learn to fly and care for themselves, and then make the long migration with them. This I doubt. I see ruby-throats over my Oswego tea bed, during August, after the young are as large as their parents. Sometime, for some reason, certain ones of a species remain after the major part of their kind has migrated, and sometimes they are found suffering and helpless with cold, as in the case of a hummingbird previously described.

If it is true that birds act subconsciously, performing the act of migration under an impulse they are forced to follow, then we must admit that very frequently they are driven to their death through following a law of their nature. For example: large flocks of several different kinds of birds chose a cold, stormy night in 1881 to cross Lake Michigan. They became chilled, confused by the icy winds, until they lost their way, were exhausted, and fell into the lake. For several days following, thousands upon thousands of birds were washed up on the shores of Lake Michigan, covering stretches of miles, where they were examined closely by many bird lovers. One man published an estimate, based on the number counted in a given space, that half a million birds lay drowned on the west shore of Michigan. Now to reverse this instance, in a lesser degree but coming under my own observation: one spring, about 1900, the birds made their northern migration too early. For ten days immediately following their arrival there was snow a foot deep, unabated cold, and zero weather, so that the birds became so sickened from hunger that they starved and froze in large numbers. They can endure extreme cold; it is lack of food that kills them. There were very few bluebirds and doves that season. The larks came into the barnyards and asked the farmers for food. A number of friends of mine fed larks with their chickens, while for those two weeks I daily carried corn, chop, and table scraps to the Valley of the Wood Robin for the cardinals and other early arrivals more tender than they. One night flight to the south would have saved the lives of thousands of the birds in my immediate vicinity, but once they had migrated they remained to starve and freeze rather than to make the short return trip, which would have saved them. It appeals to me that one could not find clearer proof than this that the birds do migrate at the dictates of a subconscious command. When they receive this command, they change locations, but nothing suggests to them that they could make a return trip for a few days and save themselves. This is a very wonderful thing, when you comprehend it, and it can be carried even further than this. Take, for example, the members of the grebe family. Grebes are migratory birds. They are capable of flight, which carries them in the neighborhood of a thousand miles, often farther, but once they have arrived at their destination they will allow themselves to be picked up by hand and killed, but they will not take wing until again moved by the migratory impulse. When they prove that they can fly by having made the long migration, why it is that they will not fly when plume hunters are gathering them up and peeling the skin from throat to vent on the living birds, is one of the secrets of nature which is difficult to learn.

Very few birds – some cardinals, for example – are what might be called walking migrants. They change their locations day by day through easy stages of flight from wood to wood; and again some specimens have been seen collecting in very small flocks and starting their southern migration much in the manner of other birds. When our birds of winter have gone farther south, there come to us from their extreme northern range such birds as the titmouse, song sparrow, cardinal, jay, nut-hatch, flicker, sap-sucker, crow, and sparrow hawk. I am sure that our mated owls remain, and I think our quail do also. Owls that have not mated and found a satisfactory home may change with the seasons until they pair and settle. It is absolutely certain that the birds farther north come as far south as my location at least in winter, for I have seen snow buntings in the woods back of the Cabin, north; and in one instance there was brought to our Cabin, south, during the winter, the body of a big snow-white Arctic owl.

Alfred Newton and Hans Gadou claim in their "Dictionary of Birds" that certain North American species, particularly limicolae, are at times found in eastern England and Scotland. The only possible explanation for this would have to lie in the fact that these birds with us breed in high northern latitudes, and in their southern migration they are blown from their course by stiff west winds, the strongest of which prevail on the Atlantic, so that the birds, unable to breast these fall gales, are blown before them to the coast of Norway, where they establish friendly relations with flocks of closely allied species and so find their way on a southeasterly course to Scotland and England, where they are recognized by dealers extremely familiar with their own species through constant handling of them. This opens up the question of whether it is not possible for reverse winds to carry European species to us. The distance would remain the same, but we are forced to admit that there are no east winds so strong on the Atlantic as the gales from the west.

There used to be a theory that birds in migration flew in wedge-shaped formation, following a chosen leader. Small birds that I have observed in migration seemed to me rather to fly in wavesthose that I recognized as finches and sparrows, robins and larks. There is more inclination among blackbirds to assume the wedge-shaped formation, but they collect in larger numbers. All the water fowl I ever have watched in migration across the open water of my lake flew in the wedge, one bird apparently leading at the point. If it is true that before they take wing the birds hold a primary and elect one of the oldest and wisest to lead them in flight, then it must also be true that they elect dozens of sub-leaders to take his place in case of accident; for on my lake I frequently see hunters shooting down the foremost birds of a low-flying wedge, in which case the formation scatters but always re-forms, another bird taking the lead. I also - have grave doubts concerning the theory of the oldest and wisest. When my birds migrate, after the old ones have performed the strenuous work of nest building, feeding their young, and have gone through the enervating process of moulting, I very seriously doubt that they are stronger and better prepared for the long flight than some of their young.

The greatest authority on the migration of birds, the one man having the widest opportunity, and who spent fifty years of uninterrupted watchfulness of bird migration, was Herr Gätke of Helgoland. His observations covered larks, starlings, wrens, and many other smaller birds, as well as plover, sandpipers, owls, and larger water birds. He states in his records that the young and the old migrate separately, generally by different routes, wiping out that beautiful theory that the old birds make their migration by landmarks they recognize, and teach the young the routes. He amply sustains the contention that birds are frequently deceived. He states the proper time for migration and then gives figures to prove that thousands lose their lives in a night through flying into a storm and breasting adverse conditions. He mentions puffins among the birds which frequently make mistakes as to when it is safe for them to migrate.

Three points of intense interest in migration are how birds find their way on nights of fog and darkness, when the theory concerning their following river valleys or recognizing bridges and light-houses is utterly untenable; the height to which they fly; and the speed. Herr Gätke's records show that the greater part of successful migration is carried on so high that while he heard the chatter of passing throngs and saw the shadows between him and the moon, he saw nothing of the birds except the weaklings and strays, which often dropped to his level through exhaustion, and paused to feed and rest. In support of the theory of high flight, Mr. G. Tennant states in his book, "Stray Feathers," that while studying the sun through a telescope," he identified as kites flocks of birds passing through his vision. This brings the nearest bird a mile above the earth, and the farthest several miles higher. These birds were not in migration; they were soaring. I mention the fact merely to prove to what vast height the birds can fly. Mr. W. E. D. Scott made a record on a night in October, 1880, in Princeton, New Jersey, of seeing through an astronomical telescope large numbers of birds, which crossed the face of the moon, flying between one and two miles in height. Among these, he positively identified warblers, finches, woodpeckers, and blackbirds. Chapman made a record of having counted three hundred birds in migration at a height of between two and three miles. In my own experience in a boat on the lake, with an unobstructed view on nights of very early spring, I frequently hear the notes of flocks of small birds passing over so high that I can not see them, but I can recognize the voices; while I also know by my own experience that on dark cloudy nights birds in migration make twice the chatter and noise that they do on a moonlight night. This probably is to enable them to keep together, to let stragglers know the position of the main flock. I frequently hear them from my sleeping porch anywhere from two to six o'clock in the morning. I think it a well-established fact that the average flight of birds in migration is at such a height that it is utterly impossible for them to see objects, which could guide their course, and I know that this is impossible on cloudy nights, when more birds seem to be in migration than in fairer weather. It is probable that the impression of numbers is obtained by the birds' chattering, caused by the fact that they can not see well in a fog so they call to each other in order to keep together. Since we know that birds unerringly cross miles of water at a height from two to three miles and find the location suitable for them, it seems that the old theory of landmarks can well be abandoned, while there is no question of the figures as to height given by astronomical observers, who are the most skilled mathematicians in all the world.

When it comes to the speed at which birds fly, it appeals to me that the scientists of former days made great mistakes. In a sustained flight at a fair height a carrier pigeon will average thirty-six miles an hour. It seems to me that the flight of a carrier pigeon, a bird of strong wing and unerring sense of direction, might very well be taken as a basis of computing the average flight of birds, at least of the pigeon and plover families. It may also be recalled that when riding on a railroad train, going at a speed of about forty miles an hour we often leave behind birds flying in the same direction. Of course such birds would not be in migration and so would not be flying so swiftly nor surely in one direction as at that time, but such a test would be of some value in determining the average speed of flight. So great an authority as Herr Gätke estimates that birds in migration are capable of a speed of four English miles to the minute. This seems perfectly incredible, as at that rate a bird would total two hundred and forty miles an hour.

In a final summing up of the migration question, I think that it is well proved that birds migrate at the demand of a subconscious impulse, that they know unerringly the line of travel to follow. Even when hindered in low flight by the blinding lights of cities and light-houses, or when turned from their course by heavy winds, unless lost and driven until they meet death, they continue their flight across long stretches of land and water, arriving eventually at their destination. I think that it will be agreed that for the most part birds that have flocked and are really in the course of long migration are at least a mile above the surface of the earth, often two or three miles. The low-flying flocks are those which have collected near to us and are not yet under headway, or strays and weaklings from larger flocks. Also, I think that it will now be conceded that the old idea of a bird's being able to make a straight sweep of a thousand miles in four or five hours is utterly out of the question. Certainly, the whole subject needs deeper investigation and more thorough study than has yet been given to it; but when the best that the human mind can do is summed up, it will probably resolve itself into this, "The stork in the heaven knoweth her appointed time" concerning when birds migrate. Their speed in flight can be determined.

One comparison which irritates me is that between birds and humans to the detriment of the birds. There is no way in which to make a fair comparison between the mentality of a creature, gifted with speech and reason, and a fowl. Recently I have heard people compare the length of time a bird droops, cries, and mourns the loss of a mate with human grief in the same circumstances. A human child, during my days of motherhood, was nourished at the breast of its mother on an average of fourteen months. In that length of time a pair of birds mate, brood, and raise three sets of four nestlings to become self-supporting. These nestlings make their southern migration, return, go through the building and brooding process, and rear their three broods of four birds each, train them to become self-supporting and ready for their first migration, while the human child is still helpless at the breast of its mother. Man's allotted span of years is seventy; five is a good average for the birds; so that they must know more when they come into this world, be ready for the ordinary functions of life much earlier, and complete them in a shorter time than does a human. Reasoning on this basis, birds are old enough when they leave the nest to know what sort of nest it is; they are old enough when left to care for themselves to know on what they have been fed, what sort of food it is, and where to find it; they know their locality before they migrate, and how to return to it or a similar place suitable to their needs; while if the few days a bird mourns a mate are to be compared with human grief, they are quite as proportionate to the length of the bird's life as is the year of the average widower to his allotted seventy. Compare a crow with a raven, a finch with a warbler, a wren with a sparrow, if you will, but to compare a bird's life with a man's is folly. This is very frequently done from the fact that birds are building homes and caring for their young. These processes are very similar with bird, beast, and human.

That a young bird, returning from its first migration, should know what location to select and of what material to build its nest is no more remarkable than that it should know when to migrate, what to feed its young, and when to leave us again. It must be conceded by any field worker of experience, however, that few young hens in their first migration build as compact and perfect specimens of architecture for a bird of their species, as old birds that have built for several seasons. This I know: the songs of yearling males are never so mellow, so high, so clear, so trilled and thrilled, so varied and original as those of birds, the feet, beak, and plumage of which indicate age. It is an incontrovertible instance of "practice makes perfect."

The sane thing to do is to admit that the birds are guided by an influence, of which we obtain hints and glimpses but do not fully understand; and whether it is called by the name of "instinct," "subconscious mind," or covered by the simple statement that the birds know matters little.

In an effort to learn exactly what the birds know in order to protect them and educate ourselves, great care should be used to keep the head level and leave the heart out of the question. The processes of nature are distinctly cold-blooded. Everywhere the strong preys upon the weak. Poetic interpretation and romancing make beautiful reading, but bad natural history. Some things which birds do are done for such obvious reasons that anyone can understand them, some we can only surmise, and concerning some we can not make a plausible surmise. It is reasonable to suppose that birds eat the food they do because when nestlings they were fed those things. Why birds of the same size, of closely related species, living in the same places and having access to the same foods, are taught some to eat grasshoppers, some worms, and some seeds, is a mystery. If they had the same food to eat, they still would remain different. You remember that grass from the same meadow makes feathers on a goose, wool on a sheep, bristles on a pig, and hair on a horse; and the same grass gives different form and feathering to the goose and the duck, eating it side by side. Certain birds, having accomplished their evolution on certain kinds of food, have gone on eating them until their structure unfits them for anything else. The seed-eaters have evolved heavy, short, sharp beaks, the fruit and worm-eaters long, finely pointed ones, the flesh-eaters strong, sharp hooks. The water feeders have broad, flat, round-pointed, shovel-like bills as the ducks, or extremely long, slender ones for probing as the cranes and herons. In each instance the beak is suited to the requirements of the bird. Further than this, certain birds are formed internally to live on certain food. Perhaps the best example is the cuckoo, provided with a flexible gizzard, lined with hair, so that it can assimilate its chosen diet of matured caterpillars without irritation. The kingfisher has such a large mouth and throat that it can swallow small fish or crabs whole and then eject the scales, bones, and other indigestible parts. Pelicans do the same. Hawks swallow parts of their prey, which they tear up, regurgitating the indigestible parts. Most of the owls swallow their prey in its entirety.

Once I saw a young crow that had been taken from a nest and raised by a boy, preparing a caterpillar for its use. It rolled the worm on the gravel at my feet until its spines were broken and then wiped it back and forth on the sawed stone walk until they were worn off. Over and over, it repeated this process until the caterpillar was a long, smooth worm. Then the crow swallowed it.

As this bird had been raised by hand, it can not be claimed that it had been taught to dress caterpillars for its food by its parents. It knew how. If one admits that this bird knew that it would make it sick to eat the caterpillar with the spines on, then one grants to the bird the ability to think and reason up to two separate perceptions on the point. It had to think that the caterpillar would be injurious if eaten whole, and then it had to think out how to prepare it for food. One might reason a degree further and say it had to recognize when the spines were removed and the caterpillar suitable for food. Nor was it stress of hunger which drove the bird to do an unusual thing, for it was well fed at home, many of the neighbours fed it, and it was regurgitating and hiding the food I was giving it around the border of a pansy bed when it espied the caterpillar.

All I could make of it was that what I was offering was unnatural food, and the bird would eat it only in stress of hunger; the caterpillar was nearer to its taste and though it was only a young bird, raised in unnatural conditions, it knew how to prepare the worm for its food. It would not do to mention "instinct" in the case, because caterpillars are not a staple of crow diet. But there are staple articles in the diet of every bird, things for which they hunger; and they do not thrive if they do not get them.

Birds pay slight attention to a dog crossing the woods and go beside themselves at the presence of a cat, so beyond all question they know which animal is dangerous to their welfare. It seems to be in the blood of a falcon to love horses and dogs. You can see the little dusky falcons, relatives of the birds formerly used by English women of rank and leisure, sweeping almost against the backs of grazing horses in the meadows, and with slight training they will perch upon the head of a dog in all confidence. I should like to see someone try to teach one to perch on the head of a cat.

When I was small, I repeatedly saw my father demonstrate that a flock of crows, feeding on corn and cut worms at a time when crows are most annoying to farmers, will pay no attention to a man approaching with a hoe, but if he carries a gun, every crow makes a sweep for a treetop out of range. You say that is simple, crows see a hoe used with no effect on them except to prepare food they like; while with a "bang!" a gun drops one of the flock.

Very well, but if you admit that, you concede to the crow the power to distinguish the hoe from the gun, to remember from day to day which is harmless and which kills, and further, to have enough knowledge and fear of death to avoid things which threaten it.

We know that birds communicate with each other by cries and calls, and of course their songs have a meaning to them, but no one ever has and probably ever will explain the concerted action of a flock in the presence of danger. With us, in similar circumstances, we say, "Something tells me!" In the same way, "something tells" the birds, but what it is, only the birds know.

Long before we know, the birds are aware of the approach of those sudden summer storms. While fisher-folk are busy casting, hunters searching the wood, and picnickers gay in the parks, the birds have their warning and silently steal away to shelter, so that when the first black cloud drifts across the sky, and the first ominous peal of thunder rolls, we suddenly become aware of how still it is, and realize that previous to our warning, the little feathered folk have had theirs and are safe. Whether there is a change in air currents imperceptible to us, whether birds of high flight see the storm clouds gathering, and their dropping to earth warns the small folk, or how they know is their secret. Any woodsman can tell you that it is quite true that the birds know first.

Slacker Cowbird knows a few things of vast importance in placing the eggs which perpetuate her species in the nests of other birds. She knows that her eggs will hatch one day sooner than those belonging in the nest in which she places them. She knows that if she places them in the nests of catbirds and thrushes of her size they will hatch at the same time as the other eggs and her young will have only an equal chance with its nest-mates. This does not suit the shirk of birdland, so she places her eggs in the nests of birds not half her size, song sparrows, indigo finches, vireos, warblers, where her young will hatch first and be twice the size of the other nestlings and so can lift their heads higher, take all the food, and eventually starve and trample to death the rightful occupants of the nest. Most small birds submit in meekness to this imposition, but a few have learned to know Slacker Cowbird and the egg she imposes upon others. Many field workers are beginning to report and to show pictures of the nests of small birds, having cowbird eggs walled under a false bottom built over them. But in this act of walling in the foreign egg I can see only conscious mind equal to the occasion on the part of the bird imposed upon, since it can scarcely be claimed that the cowbird has systematically imposed her eggs upon any one species long enough for it to have become instinctive with that species to bury the egg. My cowbird, previously described, laid five eggs, the one the song sparrow buried, one I destroyed in a vireo nest, two left in a warbler nest, and one I destroyed in an indigo finch nest. What the cowbird should learn is not to deposit her egg in the new nest of any bird, for in that case it can be buried and lost. Where the owner has laid part of her eggs and must continue to fill out the clutch at the rate of one a day, the problem becomes insurmountable, since our birds do not carry eggs around in their beaks, unless they are English sparrows carrying broken ones from nests they are destroying.

My father always insisted that the wild turkey awoke the day in the forest. I know that the coot heralds dawn in the marshes, and the robin in the fields. This has been the custom for ages, but why? Other birds join the chorus with almost the first note, why not start the music occasionally?

Probably birds know why they select a certain one for a mate. To us it looks very much as if several males surround a female, and the one which can drive away the remainder takes her. When songbirds are mated, no one knows whether it is for life or the season. If undisturbed, owls seem to live a lifetime in one hollow tree. One pair of bluejays remains about our premises every winter. Flickers seem to be in pairs in winter, and so do falcons. Cardinals and crows are in small flocks so that one can not judge. There are great numbers of dainty little folk, shy, timid creatures, with whom we reach terms of sufferance only when they are bound to their nests during brooding time, and who take to deep wood with their families as soon as brooding is over and spend the winter in the South. Whether they migrate and return in pairs is their secret; I scarcely see how anyone is going to find it out.

Perhaps bluejays know why, when they prey upon the eggs and young of almost every small bird, they give a danger signal to others the instant anything threatens them. It scarcely seems that it can be done for their protection, for as a bird protector a bluejay is a failure. Perhaps it is for the selfish reason that they do not want anything else poaching near their location.

Several years ago, when the winter was unusually prolonged and severe, a fine big male cardinal frequently came around the Cabin searching for food. He was very beautiful in a white setting, his song acceptable past belief; so I asked the gardener to take a ladder and place a big piece of bark on top of the grape arbor on which to scatter some wheat and chop every day for the bird. The English sparrows passed along the word that food was there, and soon flocks of them gathered and took all of it. So I suggested that it would be well to wait until we heard the cardinal coming, before placing his food. That set us to watching for him. We began listening for his whistle, and when we heard it, the food was placed. In a week, we were on a working basis. Every morning at nine o'clock, the cardinal came over from the Valley of the Wood Robin and perching in a large elm in the yard of a residence a square below us, sang and whistled and trilled. He came closer and perching in a hickory tree directly across from us he repeated the performance. Then he flew to a small oak on the property next west of us, closed the concert, and came directly to the grape arbor and feasted at leisure. When he finished, without uttering a note, he flew back to the Valley. At four o'clock in the afternoon he repeated the performance, always from exactly the same choir lofts. Great singers give their concerts first, and dine afterward. So did this bird.

The question of exactly how much the birds know is a vast one freighted with scientific importance. It should be handled stripped of all sentiment and devoid of all illusion, based wholly on what the birds prove they know by what they customarily do in given circumstances. It is time to repudiate what scientists who went gunning for specimens to articulate and study for the classification of species have written of bird mentality. They shot every specimen they saw before they knew its species, not to mention its characteristics. In the question of the scarcity of birds and the consequent scarcity of fruit, the work of the would-be scientist must be taken into consideration. When I read of the man who shot fifty rose-breasted grosbeaks, one hundred and fifty-two cedar waxwings, or fifty warblers to see what their crops contained, I grow indignant. Ten would furnish sufficient proof in each case and save the lives of two hundred and forty birds. This kind of work should be prohibited immediately and forever. It is wholly unnecessary to kill such numbers of birds as have been sacrificed for years. It is time to repudiate what romanticists and the fakers of city flats have been presenting to us as bird history; they have no personal acquaintance with the birds nor experience in the woods. It is time to refuse to tolerate natural history written and illustrated in parks and zoological gardens. Natural history is the history of nature, and nothing in all God's great world is so far from nature as despondent, helpless, caged birds. It is time for every man and woman wanting knowledge on the subject to go to the woods and from the unconscious birds learn what they prove they know by what they do in the daily business of living.

Added to this, I wish to register my most serious protest against the work of professional ornithologists in hastening the extermination of rare and unusual birds in their greed to secure specimens for museum collections. Museum collections at best are frail affairs, subject to moth, fading rapidly in light. Yet, let any bird be reported as rare; immediately pursuit of it with a gun begins.

Kirtland's warbler always has been the "rara avis" of our ornithology. He is an especial beauty, having a back of slaty blue with black stripes, a breast in the adult male of clear, rich yellow, sides striped with black. His history is one of the bloodiest pages of ornithology. The way of science is to shoot every Kirtland on sight. Of course, Audubon and Wilson shot all their specimens: one male Kirtland near Cleveland, "shot"; five near Cleveland, "secured"; one near Cincinnati, "shot"; one near Oberlin, "shot"; twenty-five in Canada and the United States altogether, "captured"; fifty in winter haunts in Bermuda, "taken"; two on coasts of Virginia and South Carolina, "shot." One writer states: "The pursuit of this woodland beauty, whose only offense is rarity, has been so keen that most observers have shot first and questioned afterward." Exactly! This is the history of every rare bird of the country. Of course, these methods result in the birds' "multiplying and replenishing the earth" with their species!

Then at last the nesting locality of the Kirtland, hunted from Bermuda to Minnesota, was found in Oscoda County, Michigan. Did the finder shut his eyes and his mouth and muzzle his gun, and leave this rarest bird of our ornithology to its chance to enrich the earth with its beauty and song and to help preserve our lives with its work in worm extermination? Did he? A woman would; but did the man? The report reads: "Very gratifying success. Fine series of skins, male, female, nestlings, full-fledged young, nest, and eggs." The only nesting haunt of the Kirtland ever found invaded with a gun! The rare bird once more a fugitive at the hands of science! This is a real crime, and a law should be enacted to punish it, at least in the future to prevent it. Let the word be sent abroad that the next man who kills a Kirtland becomes in Biblical phrase "a stench" in the nostrils of bird lovers, which term is synonymous with bird protectors.

CHAPTER XVII - SHALL WE PAY OUR DEBT?

ALL ornithologists have agreed for a long time past that we owed much of our comfort to the birds. To-day, it is being generally conceded that if every form of bird life were swept from the face of the earth "at one fell swoop" man could not long survive. This will seem extreme to those who have not made a study of the situation, but if anyone having access to cultivated country and villages will keep his eyes open and think out the subject to its ultimate limit, he will see that the destruction of all plant life is inevitable without the work of the birds in its preservation.

The most intimate part of my life work among the birds has been at their nesting time, when I was able to see exactly what was collected by the parents in rearing their young. All of my life I have been deeply interested in this subject because much of my life I have been in a position where I was forced to feed and care for young birds personally or to let them die; so for the birds of my location I can speak with authority as to their feeding habits, in so far as they can be followed with the eye or the field glass. It is my self-appointed task to preserve useful bird life, not to take it on any excuse whatever. But going beyond the limits of my work, comes that of the statisticians, who have carefully counted how often birds fed their young in a given time, and who have not hesitated to kill our most exquisite songsters by the dozen in order to analyze the contents of their crops. The general summing up of both branches of investigation results in the verdict that life on this planet would be insupportable without the protection afforded us by the birds against winged pests, bugs, worms, and caterpillars, larvae, aphis, and lice. With the usual exactness of nature in working out her evolution, every square yard of earth and air seems to be especially policed by these watchful, feathered servitors of ours, busy in their daily work of sustaining bird life, having not the slightest knowledge of what their work, beauty, and music mean to us.

Over the waters of my lake, during the fall and spring migration, I see wild geese, ducks, loons, gallinules, coots, gulls and grebes feeding in flocks. They keep our lakes from becoming overcrowded with fish, and feed on countless larvae and worms around the shore. During the summer, a few of the ducks – once a loon – and uncounted coots and grebes nest around the shore lines, reducing objectionable water larvae and keeping the frog production within the balance demanded by nature. Around the swampy shore line, stalk cranes, herons, bitterns, and shitepokes, keeping down the excess frog population, water-puppies, lizards, tiny soft turtles, grubs, and worms.

Over the sands race the flashing legs of rails, plovers, and sandpipers, picking up snails, larvae, spiders, bugs of all sorts, and eating the seeds of weeds and wild rice from the green majolica plates grown by the pond lilies.

Over the earth of the fields and open country go flocks of quail, cleaning up the fallen weed seeds in the fence corners, putting wasted grain to excellent use, snapping up grasshoppers and other insects here and there, helped in all this work by woodcocks, snipe, and prairie chickens, although hunters are rapidly exterminating the last. In the clover fields and meadows the larks are busy searching out wireworms and cutworms, and cleaning the breast of earth of every visible bug and worm with the assistance of bobolinks and oven birds. In gardens and dooryards, the robin is the greatest hunter of earthworms, taking uncounted thousands, also cutworms and other injurious insects comprising over one third of his food. Many people object to the robins and cedar birds because they are especially fond of cherries, but the robins are such invaluable insect exterminators that the thing to do is to plant a few Russian mulberries somewhere on your premises, and you will never again be troubled to any noticeable extent by these birds among your cherries.

At the same time these birds are busy in the open, on the floor of the woods the chewink and all members of the thrush family are scratching energetically and aiding in the preservation of the forest by cleaning boring worms and insects from the roots of the trees.

Slightly above them, in the bushes, the sparrows and finches consume untold quantities of noxious weed seed, varying their diet with countless bugs and worms, keeping to these almost entirely during the nesting season because the young birds thrive better on these than on seed.

In the higher bushes, catbirds are busy collecting worms, lice, moth and insect eggs, and eating wild berries. Here, orioles work industriously, taking moth eggs, worms, the softer bugs, and a very little fruit. The cardinal grosbeak feeds on seeds, berries, wild fruit; and when feeding young, many worms and insects. His cousin, the rose-breasted grosbeak, has the finest record of any bird in the world as an exterminator of the potato bug in its soft form, before it attains to its stiff beetle wing-shields. This alone should insure him a crown in addition to the red badge on his breast. He also eats other beetles and worms, a small amount of fruit, and a few wild berries.

In the orchards, the robins are as busy as in door-yard or garden. The orchard oriole is a veritable blessing, not in disguise, for all day long he works faithfully collecting the click beetle that few other birds will take, and destroying the tent caterpillars by the thousands. The cuckoo is so active that one pair will clean the tent caterpillars from a small orchard, taking them whole when young, dressing the spines off as the caterpillars grow older, and sucking the insides of the largest, heaviest spined ones. This is a trick not confined to birds alone. I once saw a blue wasp fly to a caterpillar crossing the steps on which I was sitting, and take a bite in the side of the caterpillar. Then, flirting his wings and giving every evidence of satisfaction, he drank from the blotch of green juice that ran from the collapsed worm. Then he flew away and told his friends; for inside of the following ten minutes, a dozen blue wasps came to take a drink of caterpillar blood. To return to the subject of cuckoos, there is a record of nine larvae destructive to black walnut found in the crop of one cuckoo; although, if he was doing such invaluable work, it surely was a pity to kill him. He should have had the freedom of the earth and a monument reciting his virtues instead. The dreaded canker worms are in his dietary list and also in that of the bluebird. Jays eat bugs, worms, berries, and alas! the eggs and young of more beneficial small birds such as warblers and vireos.

Up and down the tree trunks all day the industrious nuthatches and brown creepers, assisted by the woodpeckers of several families, search for eggs, lice, larvae, borers, and cocoons.

In hollow trees live chickadees, titmice, and crested fly-catchers, among small birds, all busy eliminating insect pests. The flicker takes beetles on trees, many ants and grasshoppers on earth.

High in the branches homes the crow. There is a strong sentiment against him because he has a bad record, based on a love of green corn, little chickens, and the eggs and young of other birds. Yet many farmers have killed crows for pulling up their newly sprouted seed corn, when the birds really were eating grub worms that were busily cutting the corn. Among poultry, a crow seldom secures a chick other than a weakling unable to escape him, and so better removed from the flock. On the other hand, a record of the field mice, small snakes, beetles, grasshoppers, and spiders that a crow takes in a week shows that he pays ten times over for all corn and young chickens he secures in a season. The worst grudge there is in my heart against the crow is his depredations among the eggs and young of invaluable small birds, birds that we can not afford to lose, either on account of their beauty, their song, or their priceless work as insect exterminators.

The gulls are the scavengers of the lake shore, the vultures and turkey buzzards of the fields and woods. Crows also assist in this work, all of which is extremely useful and beneficial in ridding the earth of a source of sickness and contagion for man.

Above both field and forest float the eagles and all the hawks. The eagles and the largest hawks feed on small wild animals, opossums, skunks, groundhogs, rabbits, moles, field mice, and snakes; also, I regret to enumerate, very small lambs, pigs, and poultry. Studying their habits closely we conclude that birds are better left alone, since their work proves of ultimate benefit to man. One pheasant farmer of one of our southeastern states hired men to help him shoot every hawk in his vicinity, only to learn a season or two later that the hawks had been instrumental in making his work a success by keeping his flocks healthful through preying upon and carrying away all the weaklings that were not sufficiently active to escape. After the elimination of the hawks, the weaklings interbred and mingled with the flock, starting disease which killed hundreds. Acting on this same theory, a certain chicken grower I know makes daily abrupt dashes among his flock and kills every chicken he can catch by hand, on the principle that if those taken were as healthful as they should be, they could escape him. It is his belief that hawks should be left alone. Either in summer or winter, a familiar figure on the telegraph wires is the little dusky falcon, commonly called the sparrow hawk, although it is my fervent belief, judging from the manner in which my song sparrows escape him, that his diet is almost altogether confined to mice, grasshoppers, and English sparrows.

During the night, my woods are full of owls, from tiny screechers as big as my doubled fist to the great horned marauders, which prey upon genuine pests, from mice, rats, water rats, and other small animals to alas! my neighbors' hens. I am sure that our hawks and owls really prefer to hunt and feed in the wild, for in five years of life where big hawks are preying on the red-wings across the lake and dipping low over our orchard and horse pasture, they never once have entered a large chicken park only a few yards away, where they daily both see and hear our chickens. The hen-house windows stand open all summer. The great horned owls banish sleep for us many a summer night, hunting through the woods and thickets around the Cabin. They sometimes alight on the roof to tear up screaming groundhogs and other prey that look the size of an average cat, but they never yet have disturbed our chickens.

The martins and swallows have the air for their province. On tireless wings, with open mouths, they sieve the air, taking millions of tiny gnats, mosquitoes, and flies, that would make life altogether unbearable for us were we compelled to live and breathe among them in their unchecked development. Smaller in size but tireless on wing and taking larger prey, I should class with the air police the gnatcatchers and fly-catchers.

Invaluable around any premises I count the work of the common house wren, which will raise three broods, averaging from six to eight young to the nest. This keeps wrens food-hunting from dawn until dark, taking every insect they see from a mosquito to a spider. The largest insect I ever pictured a wren carrying into his house was a dragonfly stripped of its wings.

It is one of the mysterious, inscrutable workings of evolution that our real safety depends upon the warbler family, its members so tiny that they are not much bigger than wrens, most of them of protective color of green and gold like the leaves of the trees, of steel and slate grey and white like the bark of tree trunks, painted, splashed, and mottled colors like the flowers, blue like the sky, or dark blue like the shadowed waters, the gayest, gaudiest, little feathered throng on earth, the almost invisible host that hunts among the leaves. They have feather-light bodies, indistinguishable among the leaves, bright eyes, tiny, pointed beaks, with which they search under and over the foliage of vines, bushes, orchards, and giant forest trees, hunting out millions and billions of insect eggs, larvae, aphis, plant lice, and tiny, newly hatched caterpillars that, if allowed to mature, would develop six inches in length. The warbler young must have insect diet. Their crops are large for the size of the birds, and the old birds keep them packed all day long. A young warbler can eat over half its own weight in insects each day and handle them conveniently.

One ornithologist kept record while a palm warbler collected from forty to sixty insects a minute to carry to its young. He estimated that the bird he was watching from his veranda took over nine thousand insects in four hours. Of course these insects were very small, but so are the wheat midge and Hessian fly; yet they do millions of dollars worth of damage to the wheat crops of one season. Scientists who have made an especial study of the work of warblers while insect collecting have kept record as a yellow-throat took eighty-four birch aphis to the minute. A chestnut-sided warbler made a record of twenty-two gypsy caterpillars to the minute, and the more agile Nashville warbler almost doubled this record by taking forty-two. Another chestnut-sided warbler took twenty-eight caterpillars in twelve minutes, and a black-and-white gathered up his twenty-eight in ten minutes. A Maryland yellow-throat collected fifty-two caterpillars in a short time. All warblers eat tent caterpillars, apple tree tent, brown tail, and gypsy caterpillars, all pests of the worst description on fruit trees and other vegetation.

The tiny host comes winging to us exactly at the right time to clean up the young caterpillars as they emerge from the eggs of moths and butterflies. How many they take in a season, there is no way to estimate. They also eat bark lice, scale insects, bark and boring beetles. They help the orchard orioles with the click beetles, while they are fond of weevils, ants, cadis flies, May flies, spiders and snails.

There can be no question concerning the value of the work of warblers in tree and vegetable conservation. While working with dozens of the big night moths of June, securing data for a book, "Moths of the Limberlost," I have had the females of some of the commonest species, Cecropia and Polyphemus, lay by actual count from three to seven hundred eggs each, while Luna and Regalis would average from three to five hundred. Placed in freedom, these eggs would have covered the undersides of leaves of orchard and ornamental trees and of hickory and walnut, among the most valuable forest trees, with millions of caterpillars, which, unchecked by the birds, at maturity would be worms measuring from four to six inches in length, each consuming his weight in leaves in a day. Were it not for the work of warblers, in spite of any form of burning or spraying, so many of these eggs would escape on the undersides of leaves that in a few years' time our orchard, field, and forest trees would be denuded of leaves by midsummer. Then the hot sun shining on the bare branches would bake them to such a bark-bound state that in two seasons the strongest of them would be dead. I have seen many single trees killed in this manner in northern Indiana and southern Michigan; and in several places I have seen whole orchards wiped out in two seasons. The warblers prove themselves our salvation above all other birds, merely by living their lives according to their evolution. It seems an alarming situation when we realize that we are so dependent upon such frail, tiny creatures with the odds so against them.

Many warblers choose extremely high nesting sites so that they will not have long trips to make in feeding their young. Others nest lower, while some select bushes only a few feet from the ground. These variable nesting locations make these birds prey to all outdoors from the crows and jays of the high treetops to the red squirrels of the middle locations and the snakes, weasels, and skunks of the ground. They suffer peculiarly from the impositions of the cowbirds, as warbler nests are so tiny that two cowbird eggs to a nest practically assure death by starvation and trampling to the warbler's entire brood. One young cowbird can crowd out, trample, and starve half of a warbler's brood. The birds are so small and delicate that they make their migration north later than most birds and in lower flight. As a result, they are particularly susceptible to cold during periods of changeable weather, while their low flight often results in their becoming baffled by the lights of cities. They are especial sufferers through becoming confused and beating themselves against light-houses. A few years ago the bodies of five hundred and ninety-five warblers were picked up one morning around the Fire Island light-house off Long Island. Storms such as I previously described on Lake Michigan are especially disastrous to them in either their northern or southern migration.

I hope I have gone into sufficient detail to prove to anyone reading this book the sum of our indebtedness to the birds. The question now becomes: how can we pay our obligation? How can we so protect and increase the birds as to raise their numbers again to such flocks as I knew in childhood, when the insect pests, which we fight each year through an expenditure of millions and much valuable time, were unknown, the work of the birds being sufficient to insure magnificent crops of large and small fruits regularly every season? So the question arises as to the manner in which we can best help ourselves by helping the birds to feed and flock with us as they did formerly.

It appeals to me that the biggest stroke which could be accomplished in their favor at one blow would be to decree and sternly carry out the

146

complete extermination of the English sparrow. It is absurd sentiment, based on ignorance of the habits and characteristics of this little villain, which allows it to go unmolested anywhere. A flock of English sparrows in a location where warblers and finches are homing means worse destruction to the birds than a plague of influenza, typhoid, and smallpox combined would mean to human beings, since a healthful human being rightly cared for has a chance of escaping the ravages of disease. Other and smaller birds have no chance whatever to escape the sparrow, which is a pugnacious little bulldog in a fight. It unhesitatingly attacks birds from the size of a robin down, breaking eggs, tearing up nests, throwing young birds from nests, eating them if they are small enough. In my personal experience, I have seen English sparrows throw the young from the nest of a robin, built where the logs cross under the roof of a veranda, the fall killing them on the floor below. I have seen them enter high bird boxes and drag out young martins and bluebirds, throwing them to their death if the young were too big to carry to their own nests for food. I have seen them enter robin nests, break the egg shells, eat all they could hold, and when they could hold no more, break the remainder of the eggs for pure mischief. Earlier in this book, I described the exquisite spectacle made by the courtship of a pair of cardinals that had selected a nesting site in the wild rose bushes over the music-room window of the Cabin, south; but I left the dnouement of that story until the present time, because I wished to use it in the strongest summing up I know how to make against the one worst menace of the birds which are working out our salvation to-day. As fast as these cardinals carried nesting material to the rose bush, and left to gather more, the English sparrows flew in, took the material, and carried it high in an elm tree in the corner of the lot, where they were nesting. In helpless rage I was compelled to stand back and see my best loved birds, these particular and peculiar friends of mine, driven from a nesting location I should have given any reasonable sum to protect. I could do nothing, since any scheme I could devise to frighten away the sparrows would cause the cardinals to desert the location. After two days of struggle, that is exactly what they did. The story is the same from every keen observer of bird life who is capable of testifying intelligently on the subject. Unless the other birds succeeded in outwitting the sparrows by some particular cleverness, nothing escaped the ravages of the sparrows at the Cabin, south, except the wren, whose house they could not enter. Aside from their incalculable destruction of other small birds in a season, it may be recorded that English sparrows are birds of disgusting habits. They do not care to exercise themselves enough to take food in a legitimate manner, preferring to feed from garbage cans, to eat the food provided for the chickens, and to steal from seed bins and granaries. They have no song; they are the lousiest birds with which I ever came in contact; they are polygamists, four or five females building a communal nest from the size of a peck measure to a bushel. They breed from February through to November, resting but two months in the year. Mr. Barrows, in his report for the Government of the United States, estimates the increase of one pair to be two hundred and seventy-five billion, seven hundred and sixteen million, nine hundred and eighty-three thousand, six hundred and eighty-nine in ten years. In the face of such a record I am surely speaking advisedly when I say that to-day they constitute the one greatest menace to our best form of timber and vegetable conservation, which is stringent bird protection. I sincerely hope that every State in the Union will make it a misdemeanor for any person to be found harboring English sparrows on their premises. Of all the foolish sentiment that was ever fostered to the detriment of our welfare in this country, the sentiment which protects "the dear, little English sparrow" is the most foolish. I should exactly as soon protect "a dear, little" copperhead or coral snake.

After sparrows, I should count the cowbird as the next worst menace to other bird life, and I unhesitatingly urge the complete extermination of every flock of cowbirds in existence. Here, again, it is sentiment of the most foolish and disastrous kind, which will protect a bird of no value in any way on earth, a songless bird of disgusting habits, with absolutely nothing to its credit except the extermination of a few grass-hoppers, to which the lark and bobolinks could effectively attend in its absence. When I recall that in my own experience in photographically reproducing the life history of one of these birds, I offered incontrovertible proof that she killed three masked warblers, two red-eyed vireos, and one blue finch, I feel amply justified in demanding her execution, as well as that of her tribe, spending their lives in similar disastrous work. If each female of a flock of over two hundred, to which this bird belonged, had an equal record, which is only fair to suppose, then on one half-mile stretch of the Wabash river bank, six hundred birds of beautiful plumage and exquisite song, invaluable to us as insect exterminators were wiped out by the cowbirds of this small flock; while, if these cowbirds averaged four eggs each, there were four hundred of these pests to take the places of the finches and warblers. This estimate is conservative, because my cowbird laid five eggs, the first of which was walled in the bottom of the nest of the song sparrow, as previously described. If I have any influence whatever, I shall most earnestly use it in advocating the complete extermination of cow-birds and English sparrows. As a matter of justice to exquisite little creatures, upon whom all of us are dependent, and as a matter of self-preservation, I urge that this matter be gone into strenuously and immediately.

The next most serious menace to our insectivorous birds, I should say is the depredations of other birds, such as crows, hawks, jays, and owls. Here we are helpless; nature must preserve her own balance. We can not interfere to any great extent. These creatures evolved together, and if left to themselves, they will keep the equation. I do make it a rule, which I advise everyone to follow wherever it is possible: give the insectivorous songbird the benefit of the doubt, protect it wherever and however possible; at the same time, my strongest displeasure is waiting for the head of anyone who touches my great horned owls, my chicken hawksI can not even allow the killing of the jays.

Because I love the birds more, it necessarily follows that I love cats less. From my point of view, I prefer to dispense with the work of a cat and solve the mouse problem with a trap rather than to have cats around; since they would spend much of the day and all of the night feeding upon beneficial birds, the song and beauty of which I adore.

I should strongly recommend a fair-sized, pliant switch for the back of the small boy or girl who deliberately destroys a bird's nest after having been carefully taught the reason for the protection of all beneficial birds. When it comes to the gunner who takes deliberate aim at an exquisite songbird, merely to test his skill, I consider him one of the most selfish, ignorant, and disgusting creatures that come within my knowledge. Sentiment on this subject is now so strong and law so stringent that these outrages are seldom perpetrated any more, but it was the body of a cardinal grosbeak, used as a target by a conscienceless hunter, which drove me to the outburst of indignation that resulted in my first book, "The Song of the Cardinal."

And I have a complaint against scientific ornithological workers that I feel it is only fair and just to the birds that I should bring forward. I realize that Audubon did a great work when he classified the birds of a continent and brought from the forests specimens of practically every bird of the United States; but at the same time, it seems to me that his records are unnecessarily bloody, that he might have accomplished equal results and killed far fewer birds. When we come to the records of scientists making up reports for the Government or for any cause whatever, I think the butchery in which they indulge is absolutely inexcusable. I can see a reason for killing ten rose-breasted grosbeaks to find if each of them has potato bugs in its crop; I can see positively no excuse for killing fifty-two for the same reason; and when the record runs from fifty-two to one hundred and fifty-two among our rarest and most beautiful birds of song on the excuse that the contents of their crops must be examined or their skins mounted for collections, I protest vigorously. Here too, the law, which is so watchful over matters of infinitely less importance to our welfare, should take a hand and specify that hereafter only the very smallest number consistent with proving a point essential to our welfare should be killed.

These things, the Government should immediately take in hand, in the matter of at least partial payment of our debt to the birds. To go further than that, each man, woman, or child who loves music, beauty, and grace, who loves fruit and flowers, gardens and forests, may do some small share consistent with his means and location. It is always possible to give a high degree of protection to the birds that seek your good graces when they locate their nests on your premises. Shield them from cats, squirrels, other birds, and willful children to the best of your ability. Put up all the boxes, old gourds, cans, dippers, any protective nesting shelter you can furnish for them. A prothonotary warbler, a thing of gold and bubbling song, passed close by a ten-dollar bird box, when it nested in my bait can on our dock last summer. The birds do not in the least object to tin cans and the crudest boxes or hollow limbs placed for their use. If you have a small waste place, where a handful of hemp seed can be sowed in spring and seed raised to add to suet and meat bones for the birds of winter, that will be a great help, since the seed is very rich in oil and a warming food for birds.

Neltje Blanchan especially requested me to urge in the writing of this book that every bird lover plant a few, low growing, thickly leaved evergreens for winter sleeping quarters for the birds, among the larger trees, junipers and red cedars, among the smaller, the cypresses and arbor vitae, these to be put in the places deemed most sheltered and convenient for winter quarters. To this, I add the plea that in every convenient corner you set a Russian mulberry as old as possible to begin with, and in a short time your complaints against the birds for taking your cherries and strawberries will be so reduced as to be negligible.

A recently published estimate of the average lifetime of birds allots to a wren three years, a thrush ten, a robin twelve, a lark thirteen, a blackbird twelve, a goldfinch fifteen, a canary fifteen, a pigeon twenty, a crane twenty-four, a sparrow hawk forty, a crow fifty, a heron fifty-nine. This gives to the birds in which we are most interested a very short span of life. It is in our power to make this life longer and safer for those of our birds, upon which we are most dependent, those to which we owe the things of life we prize most highly. While all of us are in softened mood and of a will to rectify many of the existing evils which we have endured for years, this question comes up among many other questions of not nearly so much spiritual and economic importance. In the writing of this book I have done my best. Now is the time for concerted action on the part of everyone who reads it. Shall we pay our debt to the birds?

INDEX OF BIRD IDENTIFICATIONS

- Grebe, Podilymbus podiceps.
- Grosbeak, Cardinal, Cardinalis cardinalis cardinalis.
- Grosbeak, Black-headed, Zamelodia melanocephala.
- Grosbeak, Evening, Hesperiphona vespertina vespertina.
- Grosbeak, Rose-breasted, Zamelodia ludoviciana.
- Gull, Pagophila alba.
- Hawk, Chicken, Accipiter cooperi.
- Hawk, Red-shouldered, Buteo lineatus lineatus.
- Hawk, Sparrow, Falco sparverius sparverius.
- Heron, Blue, Ardea herodias herodias.
- Hummingbird, Ruby-throated, Archilochus colubris.
- Indigo-bird, Passerina cyanea.
- Junco, Junco hyemalis hyemalis.
- Killdeer, Oxyechus vociferus.
- Kingbird, Tyrannus tyrannus.
- Kingfisher, Ceryle alcyon.
- Kinglet, Ruby-crowned, Regulus calendula calendula.
- Knot, Tringa canutus.
- Lark, Pipit, Anthus ludovicianus (Studor's "Birds of North America.")
- Linnet (Any greenish sparrow or warbler about the size of a goldfinch, miscalled "linnet" by country people, probably after the European linnet bred with canaries).
- Loon, Gavia inmer.
- Martin, Progne subis subis.
- Meadowlark, Sturnella magna magna.
- Mockingbird, Southern, Mimus polyglottos polyglottos.
- Nighthawk, Chordeiles virginianus virginianus.
- Nuthatch, Sitta carolinensis carolinensis.
- Oriole, Baltimore, Icterus galbula.
- Oriole, Orchard, Icterus spurius.
- Oven-bird, Seirus aurocapillus.
- Owl, Arctic, Bubo virginianus subarcticus.
- Owl, Barred, Strix varia varia.
- Owl, Barn, Strix pratincola.
- Owl, Great Horned, Bubo virginianus virginianus.
- Owl, Screech, Otus asio asio.
- Pelican, Pelecanus erythrorhynchos.

- Pewee, Myiochanes virens.
- Pheasant (Ring-necked). Phasianus torquatus (Reed's "Bird Guide").
- Phoebe, Sayorius phoebe.
- Pigeon (Rock Dove), Columbidae livia (Newton's "Dictionary of Birds").
- Pigeon, Wild, Ectopistes migratorius,
- Plover, Golden, Charadrius dominicus.
- Prairie Chicken, Tympanuchus americanus.
- Puffin, Fratercula arctica.
- Quail, Colinus virginianus virginianus.
- Rail, King, Rallus elegans.
- Raven, Corvus corax corax.
- Redstart, Setophaga ruticilla.
- Robin, Planesticus migratorius migratorius.
- Sandpiper, Pisobia fuscicollis or Pisobia minutilla.
- Sapsucker, Sphyrapicus varius varius.
- Shitepoke, Butorides virescens virescens.
- Shrike, Lanius ludovicianus ludovicianus.
- Skylark (non-resident) Alauda arvensis
- Snipe, Gallinago delicata.
- Sparrow, Chipping, Spizella passerina passerin-.
- Sparrow, English, Passer domesticus (Coues).
- Sparrow, Song, Melospiza melodia melodia.
- Sparrow, White-throated, Zonotrichia albicollis.
- Starling, Sturnus vulgaris.
- Summer Yellow-bird, Dendroica aestiva aestiva.
- Swallow, Barn, Hirundo erythrogastra.
- Swallow, Chimney, Chaetura pelagica.
- Swift. See Swallow, Chimney.
- Tanager, Searlet, Piranga erythromelas.
- Thrasher, Brown, Toxostoma rufum.
- Thrush, Hermit, Hylocichla guttata pallasi.
- Thrush, Wood, Hylocichla mustelina.
- Titmouse, Ba-lophus bicolor.
- Turkey, Wild, Meleagris gallopavo silvestris.
- Vireo, Red-eyed, Vireosylva olivavea.
- Vireo, Warbling, Vireosylva gilva gilva.

- Vulture, Black, Catharista urubu.
- Warbler, Bay-breasted, Dendroica castanea.
- Warbler, Black-and-white, Mniotolta varia.
- Warbler, Blackburnian, Dendroica fusca.
- Warbler, Blue-winged, Vermivora pinus.
- Warbler, Cerulean, Dendroica cerulca.
- Warbler, Chestnut sided, Dendroica pennsylvanica.
- Warbler, Green. (See Warbler, Prairie.)
- Warbler, Hooded, Wilsonia citrina.
- Warbler, Kirtlands, Dendroica kirtlandi.
- Warbler, Magnolian, Dendroica magnolia.
- Warbler, Mourning, Oparorius philadelphia.
- Warbler, Nashville, Vermivora rubricapilla rubricapilla.
- Warbler, Palm, Dendroica palmarum palmarum.
- Warbler, Prairie (Black-masked Warbler), Dendroica discolor.
- Warbler, Prothonotary, Protonotaria citrea.
- Warbler, Yellow-Pine, Dendroica vigorsi.
- Warbler, Yellow-throated, Dendroica dominica dominica.
- Wax-wing, Cedar, Bombycilla cedrorum.
- Whippoorwill, Antrostomus vociferus vociferus.
- Woodcock, Philohela minor.
- Woodpecker, Downy, Dryobates pubescens medianus.
- Woodpecker, Red-headed, Melanerpes erythropcephalus.
- Wren, Troglodytes adon adon.
- Yellowhammer (Flicker), Colaptes auratus auratus.
- Yellow-throat, Maryland, Geothlypis trichas trichas.

Made in the USA
Columbia, SC
11 March 2020